EUROPE/AMERICA
5

THE CONVENTIONAL DEFENSE OF EUROPE:
NEW TECHNOLOGIES AND NEW STRATEGIES

EUROPE/AMERICA
5

THE CONVENTIONAL DEFENSE OF EUROPE:
NEW TECHNOLOGIES AND NEW STRATEGIES

Andrew J. Pierre, Editor

Andrew J. Pierre
Richard D. DeLauer
François L. Heisbourg
Andreas von Bülow
General Sir Hugh Beach

COUNCIL ON FOREIGN RELATIONS
58 East 68 Street, New York, N.Y. 10021

COUNCIL ON FOREIGN RELATIONS BOOKS

The Council on Foreign Relations, Inc., is a nonprofit and nonpartisan organization devoted to promoting improved understanding of international affairs through the free exchange of ideas. The Council does not take any position on questions of foreign policy and has no affiliation with, and receives no funding from, the United States government.

From time to time, books and monographs written by members of the Council's research staff or visiting fellows, or commissioned by the Council, or written by an independent author with critical review contributed by a Council study or working group are published with the designation "Council on Foreign Relations Book." Any book or monograph bearing that designation is, in the judgment of the Committee on Studies of the Council's board of directors, a responsible treatment of a significant international topic worthy of presentation to the public. All statements of fact and expressions of opinion contained in Council books are, however, the sole responsibility of the author.

Copyright © 1986 by the Council on Foreign Relations, Inc.
All rights reserved.
Printed in the United States of America.

This book may not be reproduced, in whole or in part, in any form (beyond that copying permitted by Sections 107 and 108 of the U.S. Copyright Law and excerpt by reviewers for the public press), without written permission from the publishers. For information, write Publications Office, Council on Foreign Relations, Inc., 58 East 68th Street, New York, N.Y. 10021.

Library of Congress Cataloging-in-Publication Data

The Conventional defense of Europe.

(Europe/America ; 5)
1. Europe—Defenses. 2. North Atlantic Treaty Organization. 3. Warfare, Conventional. I. Pierre, Andrew J. II. Council on Foreign Relations.
III. Series.
UA646.C6749   1986   355'.03304   86-8869
ISBN 0-87609-015-3

The Project on European-American Relations

Relations between Western Europe and the United States have become more turbulent in recent years. Divergences in interests and perceptions have grown. Many are questioning the fundamental assumptions of the postwar period. There is a broad consensus that the European-American relationship is in a state of transition.

A new generation is emerging and a number of social and cultural changes are under way that are also contributing to this transition. While our common heritage and values set limits on how far we may drift apart, there is an increasing recognition of the divergences between the United States and Europe on such critical issues as defense and arms control, policy toward the Soviet Union, East-West trade and technology transfer, West-West economic relations, North-South issues, and problems outside the NATO area. The challenge for statesmen will be to manage the differences—and where possible create a new Western consensus—in such a way as to enable the Alliance to adapt to new circumstances while preserving its basic character.

The relatively simple world of the postwar period is gone. Americans today appear to have less understanding of European perspectives and Europeans less appreciation of American views. There is much handwringing about the trans-Atlantic malaise, but less constructive thinking about how to manage and, where possible, reduce our differences.

The project is designed to identify and clarify the differences in interests and perspectives affecting critical issues in the European-American relationship, thereby enhancing understanding across the Atlantic. Approximately three issues per year are selected for examination on a rolling basis over a three-year period. The issues are those that are most likely to create friction in the period ahead.

A short book is published on each issue. European and American authors with points of view that differ from each other but represent important strands of thought in their respective societies contribute analyses of the problem and offer their policy prescriptions. We hope that by disaggregating the issues in this manner, we can make a constructive contribution to the Atlantic debate.

An advisory group of Council members, with the participation of European guests, helps to choose the issues and discusses the ideas in the manuscripts prior to publication. They are, however, in no way responsible for the conclusions, which are solely those of the authors.

We would like to thank the Rockefeller Foundation, the Andrew W. Mellon Foundation and the German Marshall Fund of the United States for their assistance in supporting this project.

Cyrus R. Vance

Advisory Group
Project on European-American Relations

Cyrus R. Vance, *Chairman*
Robert D. Hormats, *Vice-Chairman*
Andrew J. Pierre, *Director of Project*
Kay King, *Assistant Director of Project*

David L. Aaron
George W. Ball
Seweryn Bialer
John Brademas
Hodding Carter, III
Robert F. Ellsworth
Murray H. Finley
Richard N. Gardner
Stanley Hoffmann
Robert E. Hunter
Irving Kristol
Jan M. Lodal
Charles S. Maier
Robert S. McNamara
Harald B. Malmgren
Robert E. Osgood
Maynard Parker

William R. Pearce
Robert V. Roosa
Nathaniel Samuels
J. Robert Schaetzel
John W. Seigle
Marshall D. Shulman
Robert B. Silvers
Anthony M. Solomon
Helmut Sonnenfeldt
Joan E. Spero
Ronald Steel
Fritz Stern
John R. Stevenson
John H. Watts, III

Paul H. Kreisberg, *ex officio*

The editor would like to thank Steven L. Canby; Col. David EK Cooper, USA; Col. K. Scott Fisher, USAF; Stephen J. Flanagan; Col. Bruce M. Freeman, USAF; Alton Frye; Michael R. Gordon; Ted Greenwood; William E. Hoehn, Jr.; Ken Hollander; William G. Hyland; Catherine M. Kelleher; Lt. Gen. Richard D. Lawrence, USA; Michael E. Mandelbaum; Barry R. Posen and James Tegnelia for their assistance in planning or commenting on the manuscripts. He would also like to thank Moira Coughlin, Meg Hardon, David Kellogg, and Rob Valkenier for their assistance in the production of this book.

The Project on European-American Relations is under the auspices of the Council's Studies Program.

Already published:
Nuclear Weapons in Europe, edited by Andrew J. Pierre, with contributions by William G. Hyland, Lawrence D. Freedman, Paul C. Warnke and Karsten D. Voigt.

Unemployment and Growth in the Western Economies, edited by Andrew J. Pierre, with contributions by Marina v.N. Whitman, Raymond Barre, James Tobin and Shirley Williams, and an introduction by Robert D. Hormats.

Third World Instability: Central America as a European-American Issue, edited by Andrew J. Pierre, with contributions by Fernando Morán, Irving Kristol, Michael D. Barnes, Alois Mertes and Daniel Oduber.

A Widening Atlantic?: Domestic Change and Foreign Policy, edited by Andrew J. Pierre, with contributions by Ralf Dahrendorf and Theodore C. Sorensen.

Contents

Andrew J. Pierre
Introduction   1

Andrew J. Pierre
Enhancing Conventional Defense: A Question of Priorities   9

Richard D. DeLauer
Emerging Technologies and their Impact on the Conventional Deterrent   40

François L. Heisbourg
Conventional Defense: Europe's Constraints and Opportunities   71

Andreas von Bülow
Defensive Entanglement: An Alternative Strategy for NATO   112

General Sir Hugh Beach
On Improving NATO Strategy   152

About the Authors

Andrew J. Pierre is a Senior Fellow at the Council on Foreign Relations and the Director of the Project on European-American Relations. Formerly on the staff of the Brookings Institution and the Hudson Institute, he has taught at Columbia University. In addition, he served with the Department of State as a Foreign Service Officer in Washington and abroad. Mr. Pierre is the author of *The Global Politics of Arms Sales, Nuclear Politics: The British Experience with an Independent Strategic Force, Nuclear Proliferation: A Strategy for Control,* and other works.

Richard D. DeLauer is President of the Orion Group. From 1981 to 1984, he served as Under Secretary of Defense for Research and Engineering. Prior to his government service, Mr. DeLauer was with TRW, Inc. as Executive Vice President from 1970 to 1981 and as a Vice President and General Manager with TRW Systems Group from 1965 to 1970. He also served in the Navy from 1943 to 1958 as an aeronautical engineering officer. Mr. De Lauer is the co-author of *Nuclear Rocket Propulsion* and *Fundamentals of Nuclear Flight*.

François L. Heisbourg is a vice president of the French electronics firm Thomson. As a member of the French diplomatic corps, he served as international security adviser to the Minister of Defense from 1981 to 1984. He was previously posted in New York as First Secretary in charge of international security issues at the French Mission to the United Nations from 1979 to 1981. He was also a member of the Foreign Ministry's Policy Planning Staff from 1978 to 1979 and an assistant to the Director of the Economics Department at the Foreign Ministry from 1977 to 1978. He is the co-author of *La Puce, les Hommes et la Bombe*.

Andreas von Bülow has been a member of the Bundestag since 1969, where he is currently head of the Social Democratic Party's Commission on Security Policy. He served as the Federal Republic of Germany's Minister of Research and Technology from 1980 to 1982 and as Parliamentary State Secretary in the Ministry of Defense from 1976 to 1980.

General Sir Hugh Beach is Warden of St. George's House, Windsor Castle and the United Kingdom's Chief Royal Engineer. He served in the British Army for 40 years, most recently as Master-General of the Ordnance from 1977 until his retirement in 1981 and as Deputy Commander-in-Chief of U.K. Land Forces from 1976 to 1977. General Beach was a member of both the European Security Study that wrote *Strengthening Conventional Deterrence in Europe* and the British Atlantic Committee that published *Diminishing the Nuclear Threat: NATO's Defense and New Technology.*

Andrew J. Pierre
Introduction

Over the past several years a new consensus has developed on the desirability of improving the conventional defense of Western Europe. Underlying this consensus, however, there is an active and continuing debate encompassing widely divergent points of view on the extent to which the defense of Europe should be made non-nuclear, the means by which this should be done, and at what cost. This debate is on such diverse issues as the proper assessment of the military balance in Central Europe; the relationship between conventional defense and nuclear deterrence; the future of NATO's strategy of "flexible response" and America's military involvement on the continent; state-of-the-art weapons technology development in the United States and Europe and how it affects the trans-Atlantic relationship; East-West relations and arms control; and public and parliamentary support for defense.

The issues are not wholly novel, but they have come to the fore in new forms recently, and a new generation has become involved. This has led to the most wide-ranging and active debate on conventional defense since the 1960s, when massive retaliation was abandoned and flexible response adopted. For the moment the Strategic Defense Initiative has captured the headlines, but conventional defense is also likely in the coming years to pinch pocketbooks and fray nerves.

Perhaps the most significant consequence in Western Europe of the years of acrimony over the placement of cruise missiles and Pershing IIs has been the creation of severe anxieties over the use of nuclear weapons in the defense of the continent. Even without the NATO deployments, there was bound to be growing discomfort as it dawned on the Europeans that, with the consolidation of Soviet-American nuclear parity, it was in the interest of the United States to diminish its "nuclear exposure" in Europe—i.e., to seek ways to reduce reliance on nuclear weapons. Such anxieties and concerns have drawn attention to conventional defense, to the notion that non-nuclear forces could be used either to deter a conflict or to delay recourse to nuclear use. The logical consequence of the much debated no-first-use principle has always been a requirement to strengthen conventional forces, although some who espoused no-first-use have been more than reluctant to accept what this would entail.

Governments and military planners, on the other hand, are concerned about what is seen as a deteriorating trend in the military balance between NATO and the Warsaw Pact. The Pact's conventional forces have been greatly improved and modernized (proportionally more than NATO's) during the past decade and this has led to concerns that the "gap" is widening. NATO's Military Committee, charged with making threat assessments, concluded in May 1985 that, given present trends, within 15 years the Warsaw Pact could successfully mount a blitzkrieg that could overwhelm NATO forces before the Alliance would have time to reinforce itself or even before the Supreme Allied Commander Europe (SACEUR) could obtain authorization for nuclear use and implement it.[1] Some knowledgeable independent analysts have come to a much less alarming conclusion, believing the overall military equation in Europe to be relatively in balance, although recommending that certain conventional force improvements be made.[2] As evidence they point to higher military expenditures for NATO than for the Warsaw Pact; to such dynamic factors as better training, more

---

[1] "Successful Pact Blitzkrieg Possible in 15 Years if NATO Doesn't Produce Better," *Armed Forces Journal International,* July 1985.

[2] See, for example, William W. Kaufmann, "Nonnuclear Deterrence," in John D. Steinbruner and Leon V. Sigal, eds., *Alliance Security: NATO and the No First-Use Question,* Brookings, 1983; John J. Mearsheimer, "Why the Soviets Can't Win Quickly in Central Europe," *International Security,* Summer, 1982.

flexibility, and greater combat effectiveness of NATO forces; and to the fact that the United States has more reliable allies than the Soviet Union. Nevertheless, NATO is seen as remaining substantially dependent upon nuclear weapons due to conventional insufficiencies. In a widely quoted statement SACEUR, General Bernard W. Rogers, has starkly warned that "If war broke out today it would only be a matter of days, not weeks, before we would have to turn to our political authorities and request the initial release of nuclear weapons."[3]

Coincident with the growth of nuclear anxieties and the perception of adverse military trends, recent years have seen a burgeoning of proposals for new conventional weapons technologies and innovative military strategies. A revolution in conventional warfare, it is argued, is at hand that could enable NATO to make up for its current deficiencies and provide the Alliance with a much enhanced, "robust," non-nuclear defense. A panoply of "emerging technologies," consisting of "smart" munitions capable of great accuracy, standoff surveillance and attack systems, conventionally armed missiles, computerized battlefield management, sophisticated command and control, etc., have been recommended for acquisition by the governments of NATO in reports of unofficial groups such as the European Security Study of the American Academy of Arts and Sciences,[4] the British Atlantic Committee,[5] as well as by U.S. Secretary of Defense Caspar Weinberger.

Almost simultaneously, although the intellectual origins were quite different, there has been an outpouring of new tactical doctrines: the U.S. Army's "Airland Battle," Allied Command Europe's concept of "Follow-on Forces Attack" (FOFA), a Department of Defense study entitled "Counter-Air 90," and unof-

---

[3] See interview with Karen Elliot House and Gerald F. Seib in *The Wall Street Journal,* June 5, 1984.

[4] *Strengthening Conventional Deterrence in Europe: Proposals for the 1980's,* Report of the European Security Study (ESECS), New York; St. Martin's Press, 1983.

[5] *Diminishing the Nuclear Threat: NATO's Defense and New Technology,* London: The British Atlantic Committee, 1984.

ficial suggestions such as Harvard Professor Samuel P. Huntington's proposal for "a conventional retaliatory" strategy.[6] What they have in common is a shift away from defense through attrition (based on fairly static operations supported by massive firepower) toward a more flexible concept of maneuver warfare. Much of the thought behind Airland Battle, in particular, can be traced back to the work in the early 1980s of the "military reform movement" in the United States, a loosely organized, bipartisan coalition that has developed fresh ideas on a wide range of military topics. It has sought to make conventional war tactics "less passive."

Both the emerging technologies and the emerging doctrines have stirred controversy and debate. FOFA and Airland Battle, for example, call for conducting "deep strikes" several hundred kilometers behind the "forward edge of the battle" in order to disrupt or destroy the second and third echelons of enemy forces. To some West Germans this is an inappropriate strategy for an essentially defensive alliance, and concerns have also been voiced about maintaining crisis stability should NATO acquire the means for a more offensively oriented strategy.

In addition, the cost of the emerging technologies would be significant. There are those who believe that it is unrealistic to assume a willingness on the part of the Alliance's member-governments to increase military spending, given current economic conditions in Western Europe and the Gramm-Rudman-Hollings type of constraints in the United States. Greater priority, it is argued, should be given to the less costly task of correcting NATO's existing deficiencies by providing for the direct first-echelon defense against a Soviet attack. The procurement of emerging technologies is certain to be politically sensitive, for the West Europeans will surely resist buying American arms without a true "two-way street." It has already posed practical problems for intra-West European arms collaboration as well as for the trans-Atlantic arms connection, although NATO began new efforts in 1985 to coordinate arms procurement through the

---

[6]Samuel P. Huntington, "Conventional Deterrence and Conventional Retaliation," *International Security,* Winter 1983–84.

Conference of National Armaments Directors. It should also be noted that the Soviets could probably respond to these new technologies and tactics by adopting similar ones or by altering their own military doctrine so as to avoid major force concentrations until the very last moment, thereby vitiating much of NATO's effort.

Any consideration of the conventional defense of Europe must take into account the ever-present American belief that the European allies are not contributing their fair share to the common burden. The U.S. deficit and trade imbalance could serve to exacerbate these concerns. There are, to be sure, sound reasons for questioning some of the American assumptions: although the United States does spend more of its gross national product on defense (the disproportion has grown during the Reagan Administration), much of the expenditure is to support its global commitments; and, as the Europeans often note, of the forces deployed in Western Europe, the allies provide 90 percent of the manpower, 85 percent of the tanks, 95 percent of the artillery and 80 percent of the combat aircraft.[7] Yet the United States still provides two-thirds of NATO's total defense expenditure, and the Europeans have generally failed to meet the three percent real increase agreed upon in 1977.

Congressional and public dissatisfaction cannot be discounted, and not too much comfort should be taken from the failure of the 1984 Nunn Amendment—which could have led to troop withdrawals—to pass by a vote of 55–41. (Indeed, the seriousness with which the Alliance took the amendment was attested to by NATO's recent decision to give high priority to the items, such as aircraft shelters and ammunition, on Senator Sam Nunn's list of deficiencies). Nunn, the senior Democrat on the Armed Services Committee, has been a stalwart supporter of NATO and, especially, its conventional defense. His goal has never been to reduce American troops in Europe, even if his tactic has been to threaten such a move as a way of inducing a greater European contribution to the defense of the Alliance. Another

---

[7] Phil Williams, "The Nunn Amendment: Burden Sharing and U.S. troops in Europe," *Survival* January/February 1985.

senator in a different political context (Alaska's Senator Ted Stevens, perhaps), might bring about a far more troubling outcome.

As a result of the heightened nuclear debate in recent years, the American public increasingly recognizes that a nuclear war, should it commence, could well begin in Europe. Senator Nunn's activity reflects a deep concern and a widening American view that NATO forces must have adequate size, stocks and sustainability to prevent rapid escalation from a conventional conflict to a strategic nuclear exchange between the superpowers.

The authors of this book have been chosen not only for their authority and expertise on this subject but also for their contrasting points of view. Each, however, is representative of an important school of thought in the Alliance debate on conventional defense. As with other volumes in this series, the reader is left to reach his own judgment. If he finds himself somewhat confused by the divergent assumptions (e.g., on the current state of the NATO-Warsaw Pact military balance) or the differing assessments (e.g., on the cost and availability of advanced technologies), let him find what comfort he can in the fact that this is a true reflection of the confusion and uncertainties regarding the conventional defense of Europe that exist within and among the governments of the Atlantic Alliance today.

Richard DeLauer, until recently the U.S. Under Secretary of Defense for Research and Engineering, views the military balance as generally adverse to NATO and is concerned about the credibility of Western doctrine should it become overly reliant on the early-use of nuclear weapons. He enthusiastically advocates that the West utilize its leadership in high technology by fully exploiting the emerging military technologies and accompanying new military doctrines of FOFA and Airland Battle. These are affordable, should be developed in collaboration with the Europeans, and hold out great promise and opportunity for rectifying NATO's insufficiencies.

In contrast, his American counterpart, Andrew J. Pierre, is a political, rather than a physical, scientist by training. Perhaps this accounts for his somewhat more skeptical approach. Eschewing technical fixes to fundamentally political problems, he sees a basic divergence in European and American perspectives on the desirable degree of dependence on nuclear weapons in Europe, and therefore on the extent to which the Europeans will be willing to improve conventional defense. In addition, he doubts that the members of the Alliance are prepared to increase their defense spending to pay for the costs of many of the emerging technologies, is concerned about a Soviet ability to respond in kind, and questions the relative benefit of deep strikes into Eastern Europe as against defending Western Europe more adequately. He also notes the concern about the impact of some of the proposed strategies upon arms control and crisis stability. Pierre supports conventional defense improvements but argues for a more selective approach and urges that decision-makers maintain a proper sense of priorities vis-à-vis other trans-Atlantic issues such as the Strategic Defense Initiative and trade policies.

Andreas von Bülow, head of the Social Democratic Party's Commission on Security Policy in the Bundestag, has been deeply involved in the defense debate in West Germany in recent years and represents a somewhat new perspective, one that is held by the center-left in a number of European nations. Attentive to Warsaw Pact weaknesses, his assessment of the military balance is substantially less disadvantageous to the West than the orthodox view. He sees a risk that advanced military technology, coupled with deep strike tactics, might lead to automatic, "pushbutton" wars, and therefore seeks a safer defense strategy. This can be found, he explains, in a more defensively oriented approach that makes greater use of militias and territorial reserves. Von Bülow also looks toward the withdrawal of American troops from Western Europe and Soviet forces from Eastern Europe by the end of the century.

A former foreign policy adviser to the French Minister of Defense and now with a leading arms manufacturing firm, François Heisbourg is impressed by the potential increased effectiveness of new weapons technologies but not unmindful of budgetary and political constraints on their full development. He notes that the American tendency to create new strategic concepts and to push them aggressively in advance of the availability of the weapons on which they are supposed to be based, when juxtaposed with European pragmatism and caution, can lead to a major trans-Atlantic disagreement over conventional defense strategy. In his view the present debate contains a good deal of "latent virulence which could flare up." Heisbourg advocates more European-initiated strategic concepts and greater intra-European arms cooperation and sees the prospects for these as based upon Franco-German rapprochement.

Finally, General Sir Hugh Beach, who brings practical experience, having served as Deputy Commander-in-Chief of U.K. Land Forces and Master General of the Ordnance, sees the need for a stronger conventional component in NATO strategy and would have it incorporate some of the new technologies; but he has doubts about implementing new tactical concepts that are overly complex. Although endorsing the FOFA strategy, he rejects the application of Airland Battle to the European context. While noting SACEUR's demurrer, he calls for a more explicit statement of disavowal of Airland Battle by senior U.S. government authorities. General Beach also urges—like von Bülow and DeLauer but unlike Heisbourg and Pierre—that more attention be given to alternative strategies of a non-nuclear, non-provocative nature based upon a decentralized defensive network and possibly using new conventional technologies. He makes the case for greater intra-European collaboration in weapons procurement and urges a *relance* of serious Mutual and Balanced Force Reduction negotiations—possibly including bans on some emerging technologies—in order to reduce the "sense of military overhang experienced by the West Europeans without diminishing the security of the Soviet Union's European empire."

February 1986

Andrew J. Pierre

Enhancing Conventional Defense: A Question of Priorities

At the heart of the question of improving conventional defense is a long unresolved debate about the extent to which nuclear weapons should be a part of NATO strategy. The adoption of the "flexible response" strategy by NATO in December 1967 was the belated recognition, after years of internal Alliance discussion, that deterrence could no longer be based upon the threat of massive retaliation if it was to remain credible. The formulation that NATO adopted in its basic document on strategic doctrine, MC 14/3, contained ambiguities that reflected a compromise between the original American idea of a "direct" conventional defense and the European preference for only a brief period of conventional war before escalating to nuclear weapons.

The Alliance's predicament began with the abandonment of the conventional force goals of 96 active and reserve divisions, plus the deployment of 9,000 aircraft, that had been set by NATO ministers in Lisbon in 1952 at the height of the Korean War. The Eisenhower Administration's "new look" strategy called for reliance on nuclear weapons to deter Soviet aggression and to make defense less costly—"more bang for the buck"—by substituting nuclear arms for expensive ground forces. Tactical nuclear weapons were introduced in Europe in 1954. But with the launching of *Sputnik* in 1957 and the looming vulnerability of the United States to a Soviet missile attack, doubts grew about the American nuclear guarantee to defend Western Europe. The complex project for a sea-based, multilateral nuclear force was designed as a response, but, with its collapse in 1964, American attentions turned to enhancing conventional forces. Then-U.S. Secretary of Defense Robert McNamara's efforts in this regard met resistance in Europe, however, because the Europeans feared that a strong conventional defense posture would detract from nuclear deterrence and ultimately lead to a "decoupling" of the American strategic nuclear forces from the defense of Western Europe.

Flexible response provides for a range of capabilities, nuclear and conventional, to enable NATO to meet aggression at whatever level it is initiated. Should an early conventional phase not be contained, flexible response calls for "deliberate escalation" to the nuclear level if necessary, up to and including strategic nuclear forces. In exchange for European acceptance of the American view that the conventional phase be taken seriously—i.e., as more than just a "tripwire," which had been the policy in the early 1960s—the United States accepted a certain ambiguity in the relationship between local conventional defense and deliberate escalation. The circumstances under which the conflict would be brought to the nuclear level were not spelled out.

Nevertheless, the United States over the years has tended to focus on a *gradual* escalation, from tactical nuclear weapons on the battlefield to limited strikes with central strategic forces to, in theory, a full scale nuclear war if all else failed. The Europeans have emphasized the seamless web of escalation, a more tight linkage, usually viewing tactical nuclear forces as a trigger to ensure full escalation rather than as a substitute for it.

Changing Attitudes toward Flexible Response and Nuclear Use

Today the doctrinal differences that were papered over in yesteryear are still with us. They are, however, becoming more complicated and troubling. The expectation that the United States would or should retaliate with nuclear weapons if a Soviet conventional attack was succeeding is increasingly being questioned on both sides of the Atlantic, as has been amply demonstrated by the considerable support for a declaratory policy of no-first-use. The debate over the deployment of the intermediate-range nuclear forces, the dispute over the neutron bomb, and insensitive statements by some U.S. officials about limited nuclear war have resulted in broadening the spectrum of

Europeans who doubt the wisdom of NATO's policy of ultimate reliance upon nuclear weapons.

Yet the alternative—enhanced conventional defense—also causes some fear and angst, often in the very same souls, resulting in schizophrenic attitudes. Whether correct or not, there is wide belief that a prolonged and full-scale conventional war—especially one fought with the more lethal conventional systems under development—could be as devastating as a nuclear conflict. On the other hand, there are also Europeans who are resisting the call for strengthening conventional forces because to do so would indicate a lack of confidence in the West's willingness to use nuclear weapons. They fear that the Soviet Union will conclude that it can risk an attack on Western Europe with conventional arms should NATO depend upon a conventional response rather than risk a nuclear confrontation. According to this viewpoint, improving NATO's conventional forces to the point of equivalence with the Warsaw Pact runs the risk of drawing Western Europe out of the protective shade of the American nuclear umbrella.

Americans, meanwhile, are increasingly noting how irrational it is to depend too greatly on U.S. nuclear weapons for Europe's defense at a time when the overall strategic environment no longer clearly favors the United States. For three decades responsible American government officials have reiterated the essence of NATO's creed—the nuclear guarantee by the United States to Europe. Similar statements appear to carry less conviction today, whether it be due to a growing sense of American vulnerability, an increasing realism, developing anti-nuclear sentiments or even general exasperation with the Europeans. For example, former U.S. Secretary of State Henry Kissinger noted that:

> The alliance is . . . trapped in a precarious combination of (a) inadequate conventional forces, leading to (b) reliance on nuclear weapons in (c) a strategic environment that makes the threat of their use, and therefore their deterrent value, less and less credible and, (d) a public climate of growing nuclear pacifism that undermines what credibility remains.[1]

---

[1] "A Plan to Reshape NATO," *Time*, March 5, 1984, p. 20.

And no less a person than Robert McNamara now states that when he was Secretary of Defense, "in long private conversations with successive Presidents—Kennedy and Johnson—I recommended, without qualification, that they never initiate, under any circumstances, the use of nuclear weapons. I believe they accepted my recommendation."[2] This statement was no doubt intended to support McNamara's views on the desirability of a no-first-use policy. His readers, however, could be forgiven if they perceive his willingness to make such a statement today as a further confirmation of the erosion, if not invalidity, of the American nuclear guarantee.

The new and broadening consensus in the mid-1980s on the desirability of enhancing conventional defense arises in large measure from the anxieties and confusion surrounding the role of nuclear weapons in the defense of Europe. It is not, it should be understood, based upon terminating the nuclear role altogether but on reducing reliance upon it, especially any early-first-use of nuclear weapons. A conventional deterrent alone would not be acceptable to most Europeans because, apart from its costs, the resulting devastation of a large non-nuclear war would be intolerable. Nor is the Alliance considering dropping flexible response; at the most it will modify it. These changes would be in practice only, rather than on paper, since seeking a consensus on a formal replacement for MC 14/3 would probably be the equivalent of drawing blood from a stone. There is support today for conventional improvements, and perhaps for altering the conventional/nuclear mix in NATO strategy in some manner. But which improvements, by what means, and at what cost they should be implemented is the subject of intense debate.

"Emerging Technologies" and "Deep Strike"

Changes in the technology of conventional war since 1945 have, on the whole, been slow and incremental. In recent years, how-

---

[2]"The Military Role of Nuclear Weapons: Perceptions and Misperceptions," *Foreign Affairs,* Fall 1983, p. 79.

ever, there has been an accelerating development in microelectronics and a variety of optical, radar, infrared and laser sensors that offer the potential of highly accurate target acquisition at great distances and in adverse climatic conditions. When incorporated in weapons together with advanced data processing systems, it may become possible to locate with precision and then destroy mobile, as well as stationary, targets up to 300 kilometers behind the line of contact. Thus the Joint Surveillance and Target Attack Radar System (JSTARS) is being developed to perform the same surveillance and battle management functions for ground warfare that the Airborne Warning and Control System performs for air combat. "Smart" anti-tank munitions with infrared guidance are being tested in the Assault Breaker program, which envisions the use of advanced standoff reconnaissance aircraft to locate targets and relay information that would result in the launching of missiles with the anti-tank munitions onto the target area. And new missiles such as the cruise medium-range, air-to-surface missile and the ballistic missile CAM-40 (Conventional Attack Missile) are being developed to carry munitions designed to crater and quickly destroy the main Warsaw Pact airfields. This is just part of a long list. Some of these systems are designed to destroy, with conventional munitions, targets that have previously been programmed for nuclear attack. Indeed, the CAM is a Pershing II missile transformed from a nuclear warhead to a package of 100 conventional submunitions.

Secretary of Defense Caspar W. Weinberger proposed that NATO examine emerging technologies at the Bonn summit meeting in June 1982. He followed it up at the year-end NATO ministerial session with a paper that identified several areas of technology with the potential to enhance significantly NATO's conventional forces by increasing target acquisition capability; providing greater accuracy and lethality of weapons systems; and improving command, control and communications. The paper also listed four areas of application: (1) defense against Warsaw Pact first-echelon forces; (2) NATO's counter-air capability; (3) interdiction of Warsaw Pact follow-on forces; and (4) command, control, communications and intelligence (C^3I).[3] The Emerging Technology Initiative (ET) has now been taken up by NATO's Military Committee and the Conference of National Armaments Directors, as well as by the Independent European Program Group (IEPG), which is working on European approaches to collaboration on equipment as part of a wider effort to provide an effective European-American cooperation in arms development.

Emerging technologies have been touted as a way of compensating for NATO's alleged weakness in the military balance in Europe, particularly its inferiority in manpower. They have also been advertised as a means of raising the nuclear threshold, not only by enhancing defense in general but also by substituting "deep strike" conventional capabilities for theater nuclear weapons. The U.S. Assistant Under Secretary of Defense for Conventional Initiatives (note the title) has recently observed: "Today we have in hand the means for a new dramatic breakthrough in the course of warfare through the exploitation of the microprocessor or chip."[4] The exploitation of these technologies, it is argued, will give NATO an effective capability to attack and disrupt Warsaw Pact reinforcement echelons. According to the British Atlantic Committee's study, *Diminishing the Nuclear Threat: NATO's Defense and New Technology*, flexible response has eroded to the point where it signifies the early use of battlefield nuclear weapons "so that this doctrine has ceased to retain much credibility as a deterrent, and needs to be replaced. Technology now offers a genuine opportunity to reform strategy and reinforce deterrence."[5]

The well-publicized and influential European Security Study (ESECS) of the American Academy of Arts and Sciences was

---

[3] See *Draft Interim Report of the Sub-Committee on Conventional Defence in Europe*, presented by Karsten Voigt to the Military Committee, North Atlantic Assembly, November 1984, p. 22.

[4] James A. Tegnelia, "Emerging Technology for Conventional Deterrence," *International Defense Review*, vol. 18, no. 5, 1985, p. 650.

[5] *Diminishing the Nuclear Threat: NATO's Defense and New Technology*, London: British Atlantic Committee, 1984, pp. 10–11.

careful in its report, *Strengthening Conventional Deterrence in Europe,* to make its recommendations within a framework retaining flexible response, but the emphasis was also on acquiring emerging technologies. Specifically ESECS urged that NATO obtain 5,000 missiles with appropriate smart warheads for the interdiction of Warsaw Pact follow-on echelons, 900 missiles for the suppression of Pact air bases and the interdiction of some 100 choke points, and 1,000 salvos of Multiple Launch Rocket Systems (MLRS) with terminally guided warheads for other needs, particularly close-in battle.[6] A supporting paper by Donald R. Cotter for the ESECS workshop on the Contributions of Advanced Technology concluded that:

1) Available and demonstrated technology can be exploited to provide new conventional deterrent options and capabilities for NATO.

2) These capabilities would fill serious gaps in NATO's conventional posture and allow less dependence by NATO on possible early use of nuclear weapons.

3) The suggested conventional mission options in counter-air, interdiction, and defeating Warsaw Pact mobile ground forces—echeloned and in contact—could be made available in the period 1986 through 1988, given a timely decision.

4) The capabilities could be had within current and programmed NATO force levels.

5) With effective non-nuclear capabilities for executing the counter-air, interdiction, and counter-ground-force missions, a shift in roles for NATO's conventional and nuclear forces could occur. Modern nuclear forces would perform the "hold-at-risk" and retaliating functions. Modern conventional forces would constitute a formidable war-fighting capability in the event of aggression against NATO.[7]

---

[6]*Strengthening Conventional Deterrence in Europe: Proposals for the 1980s,* Report of the European Security Study Group (ESECS), New York: St. Martin's Press, 1983, p. 30. A supplementary report in 1985, ESECS II, developed further recommendations.

[7]*Ibid.,* p. 250.

The advocates of emerging technologies wish to "exploit" them in the new tactical doctrines that are also emerging. "Airland Battle" was developed by the U.S. Army with Air Force participation, for worldwide applicability and has now been codified in *Army Field Manual 100-5: Operations.* It calls for seizing and maintaining the initiative in order to deny success to an aggressor's attack. While the battle goes on at the first echelon, there should be deep strikes—up to 150 kilometers behind the forward edge of the battle area—against the enemy's still uncommitted forces in order to disrupt and delay their entry into combat. The corps commander is given considerable flexibility within the overall battle plan; his emphasis is on maneuver as a means of concentrating strength against enemy weaknesses. It is the deep strike role as well as Airland Battle's combined use of chemical and nuclear forces, along with conventional ones, in an "integrated and extended" battlefield that has led to controversy.[8]

Allied Command Europe's plan, known as "Follow-on Forces Attack" (FOFA), has been developed at SHAPE headquarters quite independently from Airland Battle and is termed an operational "sub-concept." Follow-on forces are defined as those forces that have not been committed to the initial attack. As the Supreme Allied Commander Europe, General Bernard W. Rogers has taken pains to point out, it does not provide for an integrated use of conventional, nuclear and chemical weapons. Neither are *ground* forces used for attacks deep into the enemy's rear area.[9] However FOFA does envision a theater-wide targeting of "choke" points such as bridges and rail lines in Eastern Europe, as well as of massed armor and troop concentrations, in order to disrupt and destroy the Warsaw Pact's reinforcing echelons. These deep strikes are to be made by air up to 400 kilometers behind the forward edge of battle. Contrary to some criticisms that have been leveled at it, deep air interdiction is not new

---

[8]Boyd D. Sutton, *et al.,* "Deep Attack Concepts and the Defense of Central Europe," *Survival,* March/April 1984, pp. 50–70.

[9]General Bernard W. Rogers, "Follow-on Forces Attack (FOFA): Myth and Realities," *NATO Review,* December 1984, p.7.

to NATO's war plans. However up to now the means to undertake a deep strike have been lacking as the Alliance has been dependent upon manned aircraft that would have to penetrate thick air defenses. The intention of FOFA is to use emerging technologies in order to interdict and kill Soviet second- and third-echelon forces before they can become engaged in battle. NATO's Defense Planning Committee endorsed FOFA in November 1984, reportedly with a skeptical, lukewarm attitude and under American pressure. Since then FOFA has been under active study and is being refined. Much will depend upon the availability of emerging technologies for deep surveillance and strikes that the Alliance has yet to agree to adopt in order to implement FOFA.

A third plan, "Counter-Air 90", originating in the U.S. Department of Defense, proposes to use ballistic missiles armed with conventional munitions for attacking Warsaw Pact airbases. This was also suggested in the ESECS study. But since this could cause major problems for crisis stability (it is not clear how the Soviet Union would be able to distinguish an incoming conventionally armed ballistic missile from a nuclear one such as a Pershing), many Europeans have raised objections to it. Counter-Air 90 is now being studied by a special panel in NATO, but it has not been endorsed by General Rogers and its future is quite uncertain.

Six Critical Questions

West Europeans and Americans alike have had mixed reactions to the various programs and proposals dealing with new conventional technologies and new military strategies that have been made in the past several years. These proposals need to be aired more widely, in a non-technical manner, beyond the circle of politicians, officials, academics and defense experts who constitute the international security community. Enhancing conventional defense is at the core of the nuclear issue within the West. If the chances of a nuclear war can be diminished by raising the nuclear threshold through conventional defense improvements, the *hows, whys* and *at what costs* of the issue need to be better known and understood.

Although the reaction on both sides of the Atlantic has been mixed, it is also fair to say that faced with the new proposals, which are almost invariably American in origin, the dominant European response has been cautious and skeptical, while the American attitude has usually been more positive and enthusiastic. With a host of new conventional defense initiatives coming from Washington the seeds of a major disagreement are clearly present. The Alliance is now facing a divisive debate over the implications of the Strategic Defense Initiative (SDI), is increasingly uneasy about the European lag in technology vis-à-vis the United States (and Japan), and will be confronting major trade problems in the near future—all issues with which the conventional defense problem is linked. Maladroitly handled, it could become a matter of major discord.

In order to clarify the conventional defense problem six questions need to be addressed.

First, how militarily effective are "emerging technologies" and to what extent are they available now or will they be soon, as compared to the distant future?

We are talking about a wide range of technology and a variety of military systems, some of which have already emerged, such as the MLRS. But many of the weapons to be exploited in the new military doctrines, especially for deep strike missions, are not likely to be available until well into the 1990s (if decisions are now made to go into full development). The ESECS study and statements such as that by Secretary Weinberger saying that "technology is revolutionizing the conventional battlefield and offers the Alliance the high ground of increased performance and efficiency for marginal increases in development or production costs,"[10] may have been unduly optimistic. A recent study by John Burgess argues that the promise of ET does not appear as bright now as it did in 1982. Developmental delays and procurement difficulties, including major inter-service rivalries over

---

[10]*Standardization of Equipment within NATO: Tenth Report to U.S. Congress,* Department of Defense, 1984, p. 1.

roles and missions, have plagued the programs in the state-of-the-art technologies. Although ET may eventually have considerable impact, Burgess concludes that it will come later, be more incremental, and more expensive than originally planned.[11]

Questions have also been raised about the military effectiveness of some of the principal emerging technologies. Steven L. Canby has serious doubts about their operational feasibility. In a hostile combat environment, technologically complex weapons systems, in which individual functions from widely different equipment must be stitched together, are prone to break down. The problem is currently demonstrated in Assault Breaker where no demonstration has, to date, successfully brought all the functions together, including mid-course correction for deep-ranging missiles. Moreover, automated targeting and precision-guided delivery systems are highly vulnerable and prone to countermeasures. Military history, adds Canby, suggests that technological advantage is transitory in nature, readily copied and countered. Technology is neutral and should not be expected to favor the defense over the offense. NATO, he concludes, is unlikely to obtain a significant military advantage from emerging technologies for long.[12]

Perhaps because Europeans tend to be less technologically optimistic than Americans, their political leaders have been more cautious in accepting the feasibility and availability of these "miracle" weapons. NATO Secretary General Lord Carrington, in addressing NATO parliamentarians, has warned about the "dazzle" and "sex appeal" of new technology that might distract policymakers from focusing on other needs in Western defense.[13] And a disclaiming statement by the then-British Minis-

---

[11]John A. Burgess, "Emerging Technologies and the Security of Western Europe," in Stephen J. Flanagan and Fen Osler Hampson, eds., *Securing Europe's Future: Changing Elements of European Security,* London: Croom Helm, 1986.

[12]Steven L. Canby, "The Operational Limits of Emerging Technology," *International Defense Review,* vol. 18, no. 6, 1985, pp. 875–880.

[13]"NATO Warned of High-Tech Arms 'Dazzle'," *The Washington Post,* November 15, 1984, p. A30.

ter of State for Defence Procurement, Geoffrey Pattie, has been widely and approvingly quoted in Europe:

> Emerging technology is not a panacea. It is not a strategy real or surrogate. At best the emerging technologies will enable us selectively to convert what is technologically feasible into what is operationally cost-efficient and relevant. At worst, the emerging technologies can become costly potential capabilities looking for work to do. . . . I believe there are very real constraints on the extent to which, and the rapidity with which, ET can be exploited for defense purposes.[14]

Second, what priority should be accorded to "deep strike" in NATO's military strategy?

Deep strike is designed to allow NATO, after it is attacked, to carry a war rapidly and deeply into Warsaw Pact territory. New, mostly emerging technology would be used to interdict second- and third-echelon follow-on forces before they could reach the main battlefield. This is not entirely novel for NATO's wartime plans, for the Alliance has always assumed it should take the battle to the enemy by air, but there are two new elements: (a) Airland Battle (but not FOFA) calls for an offensive role for *ground* forces in the enemy's home territory, which in this case would be Eastern Europe; and (b) plans for interdiction by air in the past have been for *fixed* targets, such as airfields and choke points, rather than *mobile* targets that are well behind the battleline, making for a costly and difficult mission.

What *is* quite new, however, is that for the first time the technology may actually become available to interdict deeply, including mobile targets. Highly accurate missiles capable of striking targets deep in the Warsaw Pact from launch points well to the rear of the main battle area are being developed, as well as long-range surveillance and target acquisition systems that are capable of finding distant enemy formations and keeping track of them even when they are on the move.

---

[14]"Emerging Technology: The Need for Reality," paper delivered at *Economist* Seminar, February 9, 1984.

The main point of the criticism leveled by opponents of deep strike is that NATO's primary task must be to prevent a blitzkrieg by first-echelon Warsaw Pact forces at the forward edge of the battle area.[15] This task has become more urgent in the past several years as the Soviet Union has concentrated on improving its forward-based forces, with the aim of giving the Warsaw Pact a rapid penetration, conventional-only capability, possibly to preempt NATO's first-use of nuclear weapons. West German Minister of Defense Manfred Wörner has warned about the Pact's growing first-echelon threat, which is not dependent upon reinforcements and is designed to defeat NATO conventionally. There are thus sufficient concerns about NATO's military vulnerabilities in its forward defense to warrant placing additional resources there. What good is striking deep into Eastern Europe if, meanwhile, Pact forces are breaking through NATO front lines? David Greenwood has suggested that if NATO needs a slogan, it should be "Strike Shallow not Strike Deep."[16] The Alliance needs to concentrate at present on countering the adversary's first echelon, the 19 plus Soviet divisions in East Germany and Czechoslovakia.

NATO's principal need today is to improve the readiness, survivability and sustainability of its forces in order to hold back a Soviet intrusion and defend in depth, rather than to expend its limited resources on taking the war into Eastern Europe. General Rogers, in testimony before the Senate Armed Services Committee in March 1985, listed a number of "war stoppers"—deficiencies that would quickly force the Alliance to surrender or resort to nuclear weapons within days of an attack. These deficiencies included a shortage of munitions, spare parts, and other war stocks in which NATO does not meet the 30-day supply goal agreed upon by the Alliance ministers; a lack of adequate numbers of aircraft shelters to protect the approximate 1,500 planes that will be rushed to Europe in the first ten days of

---

[15]See Jeffrey Record, "NATO's Forward Defense and Striking Deep", *Armed Forces Journal International,* November 1983, pp. 42–48.

[16]"Strengthening Conventional Deterrence," *NATO Review,* August 1984, p. 9.

22 / *The Conventional Defense of Europe*

battle; too few aircraft to provide for adequate reinforcement; and outdated chemical weapons.[17] Unfortunately, these are rather mundane items, lacking high-tech glitz, but their critical importance has been recognized by Senator Sam Nunn who made them an integral part of his 1984 amendment. An early supporter of emerging technologies, Nunn has reexamined his priorities. In a recent interview he observed:

> If you are not going to have enough ammunition to fight 30 days, and if you aren't going to have enough essential facilities and shelters to give your aircraft a chance to do what they're capable of doing, emerging technologies become irrelevant. Emerging technologies can't possibly be expected to make up for critical conditions like running out of ammunition.[18]

Deep strike must be viewed in the context of overall military needs. New means with which to attack second- and third-echelon Warsaw Pact forces should not divert resources from the critical first-echelon line of battle, where a war could quickly be lost or NATO could be forced to go nuclear. Yet any judgment must be carefully balanced. No less a proponent of conventional defense than the indefatigable Robert W. Komer has recognized that deep strike capabilities—depending upon their magnitude, survivability and reliability—could so seriously degrade the effectiveness and sustainability of a Warsaw Pact attack as to reduce the need for other costly conventional requirements.[19]

In the best of worlds, NATO would be able to augment significantly its conventional capabilities at all levels, and deep strike would not be a diversion from the first-echelon defense. But as is discussed below, the governments of the NATO nations are not likely to increase their spending to a level that

---

[17]See Bill Keller, "NATO Chief Finds Conventional Forces Lacking," *The New York Times*, March 2, 1985.

[18]See "Nunn: More to Do," interview with Michael R. Gordon in *Military Logistics Forum*, March 1985, p. 29.

[19]"Cost and Benefits of a Credible Conventional Component," *Armed Forces Journal International*, May 1984, pp. 112–116

would obviate the need for choice. In the competition for limited resources, therefore, first priority should be given to the most dangerous threat to NATO: forward-deployed Warsaw Pact forces that could achieve a quick breakthrough against NATO's forward defenses.

Third, what would be the costs of "emerging technologies" and "deep strike" and what are the prospects of the Alliance funding them?

The extent to which NATO is able actually to implement FOFA and equip its forces with emerging technologies will be decided by a mix of political and economic considerations, of which resource constraints may well turn out to be the most important.

Even without new technologies or tactics, the costs of conventional defense are increasing. NATO is engaged in a modernization program (as has been the Warsaw Pact, but at a more rapid pace) and is introducing new weapons systems into its armed forces. The cost of advanced weapons is escalating. Jacques Gansler, a former U.S. Defense Department official concerned with weapons procurement, reports that "the generation-to-generation increase in the cost of weapons systems has been consistently rising by 5–6 percent every year, after adjusting for inflation and annual variations in the number of weapons purchased."[20] Almost invariably new defense equipment is more complex and costly than that which it replaces. Most of the higher costs for currently agreed-upon programs and missions would have to be absorbed at the same time as the additional costs required for the deep strike missions, for the latter would in the main *supplement* the present conventional forces rather than substitute for them.

The European Security Study estimated that the cost of procuring and operating the new conventional weapons systems recommended in its report could amount over a ten-year period to about $20 billion, with a possible variation of 50 percent higher

---

[20]"We Can Afford Security," *Foreign Policy,* Summer 1983, p. 67.

or lower. These costs, it was expected, could be accommodated within a level of expenditure one percent higher than the current NATO defense spending goal of three percent annual real growth, assuming that goal is sustained and extended after 1986. But this estimate has been widely criticized as too low, and the history of weapons acquisition has been that the more complex and innovative the technology, the greater the cost overruns are likely to be. General Rogers has also stated that the cost of obtaining a robust conventional capability, including some interdiction capabilities against follow-on forces, would be about four percent in real growth over six years.[21] It is not clear, however, whether the SHAPE calculations on which he based his statements included the costs of deep strike programs; a Rand study of this whole question concludes that they did not.[22]

Even though these two estimates may be optimistically low, they do state the need for sustained increases in spending if deep strike is to be achieved through emerging technologies. The wishful view one hears on occasion that the greater efficiency and lethality of advanced weapons technology will permit a reduction in numbers of weapons, and therefore in the total price tag, is in all likelihood a pipe dream.

What then are the prospects for increased defense expenditures by the Alliance countries to pay for the emerging technologies? Barring an unexpected and dramatic further decline in East-West relations, one that would result in a vastly heightened perception of the danger, they are practically nil. As it is, the European members of the Alliance have not been able to consistently meet the three percent annual increase goals set in 1977. The growth in defense spending of non-U.S. members of NATO was 2.9 percent in 1981, 2.3 percent in 1982, and 1.1 percent in 1983; it did reach 3 percent in 1984, but this was due to the reduction of inflation.

There are really two questions that must be considered: (a) whether emerging technologies will be given a high priority

---

[21] General Bernard W. Rogers, "The Atlantic Alliance: Prescriptions for a Difficult Decade," *Foreign Affairs*, Summer 1982, p. 1155.

[22] Roger L.L. Facer, *Conventional Forces and the NATO Strategy of Flexible Response*, Santa Monica, Ca.: Rand, No. R-3209-FF, January 1985, p. 65.

within the national defense budgets at their existing levels; and (b) whether defense expenditures will be increased as a whole.

Despite the support for the ET Initiative in some quarters, it is unlikely to become a very high priority within the ministries of defense throughout the Alliance. One reason, as discussed earlier, is the lingering uncertainty in Europe about improving conventional defense if it results in a diminished perception of nuclear deterrence. There are also other political and crisis stability considerations, which are addressed below, but the chief reason the support for spending on ET is likely to be soft comes from competing military requirements.

In Great Britain, the decision to buy the Trident ballistic missile from the United States has resulted in a ten billion pound sterling program that is likely to lead to deep cuts in conventional forces even without ET. The House of Commons Defense Committee reported in June 1985 that unless something changes in the 1990s, there will be "cancellations, slowing-down of acquisitions and the running-on of equipment beyond its economic lifespan." It concluded that there are bound to be serious defense cuts that are almost certain to fall on conventional equipment.[23] A University of Bradford study estimated if the cuts necessary to finance Trident were applied early to new conventional equipment, spending on it would fall by 35 percent between 1984–1985 and 1989–1990.[24] This is even taking into account projected reductions in the number of servicemen and civilians employed.

In France, also, the modernization of nuclear forces is being given priority over conventional defense and is being allocated a larger proportion of the equipment budget than before, although the nuclear component remains well below non-nuclear expenditures. Moreover, within the context of reduced conventional forces, the new Force d'Action Rapide, designed for worldwide intervention, is receiving preference. (One central role that France has in mind for the FAR, however, is reinforcement of its forces in West Germany).

---

[23]"Trident's Real Costs," *The Economist,* June 15, 1985, p. 55.
[24]*Ibid.*, p. 56.

In the Federal Republic of Germany, the cause of the problem is different but the result is the same. Because of declining birth rates, the number of potential conscripts for the Bundeswehr is expected to drop from 300,000 in 1985 to 160,000 in the mid-1990s. In order to keep the Bundeswehr at its full strength, even allowing for the planned extension of military service from 15 to 18 months beginning in 1989 as well as for some lowering of physical and mental standards for draftees, it will be necessary to offer higher pay both to attract longer term volunteers and to rely more heavily on reservists. The defense budget is not expected to rise by more than one percent in real terms, and the opposition Social Democratic Party (SPD) has called for a freeze on defense spending. It is unlikely much money will be available for the new technologies; even the on-going weapons programs, such as the equipping of the Tornado aircraft with modern munitions systems, will have to be squeezed.

As for the United States, the growth in defense spending under President Ronald Reagan appears to have come to a close. Despite the enthusiasm for the ET Initiative, it surely will have difficulty holding its own against the competing claims of the Strategic Defense Initiative, the modernization of strategic nuclear forces, the Navy buildup, and even some of the Army's other programs, such as the full fielding of the M–1 tank. All in all there seems to be a quite limited scope in either Europe or the United States for a significant shift, within available defense resources, toward conventional defense, especially of the ET and deep strike variety.

Nor is the totality of resources for defense likely to be increased in the coming years. The economies of Western Europe have still not achieved significant growth rates and that of the United States is leveling off. Unemployment in Europe remains unacceptably high, and aging populations are adding to the social welfare burden. There is a desire to reduce taxes as a means to increase incentives for investment so as to enable the industrial sector to renovate in order to compete effectively with the United States, Japan and the Third World. Under these difficult circumstances, the "opportunity cost" test that any military spending increase would have to pass will be tough indeed.[25]

Fourth, where are the emerging technologies to be produced, in America or in Europe?

The clear answer must be in *both* the United States and the relevant European nations if these new concepts are to be adopted. Ten years after the publication of the Callaghan Report, the Europeans have become very skeptical about the "two-way street" in arms procurement because so much of the traffic has been down a one-way avenue. According to a British Ministry of Defence official, when the Reagan Administration first broached emerging technology to the European allies "many feared that Weinberger's stress on cooperative programs and the avoidance of duplication concealed a new effort to persuade them to adopt American systems."[26] Although this was a misplaced fear, there clearly is a great deal of sensitivity to the question. As recently as August 1985 Manfred Wörner saw "a clear deficit in the so-called two-way street. The U.S. is not yet ready to accept the idea that we have to cooperate for the long term, although in a lot of short-term ways we have."[27]

If NATO is to implement FOFA—a task that is just beginning—it will have to do so on the basis of broad Alliance participation. It is occasionally suggested that the United States take on the follow-on forces role (mainly a task for the most sophisticated weapons) and that the Europeans be responsible for the first echelon (where manpower is more important). This two-tier approach is contrary to the common defense principle of the Alliance and should be rejected. It may be true that most of the emerging technologies to date—although not all—have been American efforts. (This is especially true of the more complex

---

[25] Phil Williams and William Wallace, "Emerging Technologies and European Security," *Survival,* March/April 1984, pp. 70–78.

[26] Facer, *op. cit.,* p. 58.

[27] See Giovanni de Briganti and Benjamin F. Schemmer's interview with Manfred Wörner, in *Armed Forces Journal International,* August 1985, p. 56.

weapons systems designed for second-echelon, deep interdiction.) However, as the Burgess survey points out, the lack of a coordinated Alliance-wide emerging technology procurement policy has already spawned a wide range of overlapping systems.[28] To the extent that the United States now has a dominant position in the development of the more advanced emerging technology weapons, it would be desirable to obtain significant European participation in production in order to achieve some balance in procurement, he suggests. Another European concern, which needs to be allayed, is that the Reagan Administration's more restrictive policies on the transfer of technology would result in the allies only being able to participate in the less interesting technologies.

We may now be at the point where we have a fresh opportunity, with emerging technologies (to the extent that they are actually funded), to create a new, cooperative trans-Atlantic relationship in weapons technology. An excellent, insufficiently noticed, move in this direction can be found in the amendment introduced in 1985 by Senator Nunn that would allocate $200 million for cooperative weapons research between the United States and its European allies for advanced conventional arms and another $50 million for "side-by-side" comparison testing of weapons manufactured in Europe and the United States. The amendment would also require the Pentagon to consider arms cooperation possibilities at an early procurement stage. Meanwhile the Europeans are making some progress toward harmonizing their weapons research programs in the IEPG, which includes France, but which operates in the general framework of NATO. Although the history of intra-European weapons collaboration has been discouraging, there is a new ferment of interest. This had led to the revival of the Western European Union, the suggestion that the European Economic Community become involved in this field, and discussion of expanding Franco-German cooperation.[29] In addition, SDI, EUREKA, and

---

[28]Burgess, *op cit.*

[29]For contrasting points of view see Robert McGeehan, "European Defence Cooperation: A Political Perspective," *The World Today*, June 1985; and William Wallace, "European Defence Cooperation: The Reopening Debate," *Survival*, November/December 1984.

worries about Europe's technological "lag" are all likely to create pressures for collaboration of various types that might lead to improving conventional weapons cooperation. So there are grounds for hope, if not for optimism.

Fifth, what will be the nature of the Soviet response?

Predictions of Soviet behavior are hazardous, and there is already a growing debate among Western analysts of Soviet military policy on the likely nature of the Soviet response. At the political level, Moscow could well launch a major propaganda campaign designed to create opposition within NATO countries to what the Soviets could characterize as a new offensive strategy, which in their view will increase arms spending, heighten tensions, fuel the arms race, and destabilize Europe—all while serving American interests by keeping a war limited to European soil. When FOFA was adopted by the Military Committee of NATO in November 1984, it was denounced in *Pravda* as a dangerous new doctrine that the Pentagon was imposing upon the European allies. Whenever it suits the Soviets, the volume on these themes could be turned up several notches so that it even hits the decibel level reached just before the initial deployments of intermediate-range nuclear forces in Europe. There will be ample opportunity for the Soviets to denounce the aggressiveness of deep strike if and when new Western capabilities for attacking the second echelon are introduced into NATO forces. It is noteworthy that Soviet leader Mikhail Gorbachev's January 1986 arms control proposal called, for the first time, for "a ban on the development of non-nuclear weapons based on new physical principles, whose destructive capacity is close to that of nuclear arms."[30]

Equally important, there are a number of significant countermeasures that the Soviet Union could undertake. For example, Moscow could increase the combat power of the Warsaw Pact first echelon by assigning more Soviet divisions to East Germany and Czechoslovakia, thus further strengthening the Pact's

---

[30]TASS press release, January 15, 1986, New York, U.S.S.R. Mission to the United Nations.

ability to make a rapid breakthrough into NATO territory and forcing a political collapse of NATO before a decision to use nuclear weapons could be made. Another countermeasure the Soviets could undertake would be to increase the speed and ease with which Soviet follow-on forces could be moved forward into battle, thus reducing the potential damage resulting from NATO's interdiction efforts. A British analyst of Soviet military affairs argues that the Soviets have already rewritten their operational plans so as to use their new "operational maneuver groups" to penetrate NATO forces quickly and get behind the line of battle. The aim of these groups would be to disrupt communications and destroy key targets such as nuclear delivery systems so as to lead to a quick end to the war on the battlefield, before escalation to the nuclear level. According to this view, the Warsaw Pact's new emphasis on a single major operational echelon makes FOFA's strategy of deep strike interdiction unnecessary, even irrelevant.[31] General Rogers has made it evident he does not agree with this analysis.

There is no reason, moreover, why emerging technologies should remain a Western monopoly. Marshal Nikolai V. Ogarkov, former Chief-of-Staff of the Soviet armed forces, has made it clear that he takes them most seriously as a "qualitative leap," making conventional systems "incomparably more destructive" than before and sharply extending the zone of combat operations.[32] In addition, he is known to favor increased Soviet investment in advanced conventional weapons technology. Since the Soviet Union will also be facing a demographic squeeze in the next decade, and having traditionally had armed forces that are heavily manpower dependent, the Soviets may have their own reasons for being attracted to high-tech weaponry. A detailed

---

[31]See Christopher N. Donnelly, "Soviet Operational Concepts in the 1980s," in *Strengthening Conventional Deterrence in Europe* (ESECS), *op. cit.*, pp. 105–136; and "The Development of the Soviet Concept of Echeloning," *NATO Review*, December 1984.

[32]Interview with MSU N.V. Ogarkov in *Krasnaya Zvezda*, reprinted in Foreign Broadcast Information Service (FBIS), Washington, D.C., May 9, 1984, section III, p. R 19.

and balanced study undertaken by officers at the U.S. National Defense University reasons that the Soviet Union in the short run is unlikely to see any urgent need to alter its force structure in response to new NATO technologies and military concepts. The Soviets will continue to have considerable numerical advantages, which coupled with on-going modernization and what they regard as the superior moral and fighting qualities of their troops, will in their minds assure the Warsaw Pact of a decisive advantage on the battlefield. For the long run, however, the Warsaw Pact "probably sees Airland Battle, Deep Attack concepts, and especially several important new Western technologies as very threatening developments, and it is therefore likely to adjust operational planning, force development and 'preparation of the battlefield' to meet the challenge."[33] Why should the West expect anything else?

Sixth, what would be the impact of the new technologies and new strategies upon East-West relations and on stability during a crisis?

There are a number of considerations of this nature that are important, because they are potentially very troublesome politically, and therefore they need to be carefully weighed.

Deep strike concepts, even by their very title, appear to some as unnecessarily provocative. NATO is, after all, a defensive alliance intended to provide reassurance and deterrence and a restoration of the *status quo ante* should there be a conflict. Even if retaliatory strikes across the border were always part of NATO's war plans, the adoption of new longer range weaponry and the explicit statement of such a strategy in peacetime are quite another matter in political terms. Sensitivities to this are especially acute in the Federal Republic of Germany. As Josef Joffe, a strong West German supporter of the Western Alliance, has observed in criticizing the new conventional war ideas:

> Nor will the West Europeans swallow the political implications of such a posture. . . . There is now a shadowy political

---

[33]Sutton, *et al., op. cit,* p. 63.

system defined not only by all kinds of economic and political ties but also by a West European *prise de conscience* that regards the East Europeans not as enemies but as hapless victims and even tacit allies.... With the Federal Republic in the vanguard, the West Europeans will fight tooth and nail against a doctrine that would seek to deter the Soviets by threatening the East Europeans and hence the very ethos of Ostpolitik and détente.[34]

Although the Christian Democratic government in Bonn has held back from strongly opposing the new American concepts, it has not been actively supporting them either, calling rather for further study and analysis. The SPD, on the other hand, has been more openly critical. There is a risk, as General Graf von Baudisson (Ret.) has pointed out, that the purported offensive nature of the new doctrine will be used by Soviet propaganda as proof of the menace of Western "revanchisme."[35] Should the notion become widely accepted on the European Left that NATO is moving toward an inappropriate offensive doctrine this could render still more difficult the maintenance of public, and therefore political, support for the Alliance.

Because it has received a considerable amount of attention in both Europe and the United States, at least brief mention must be made of Professor Samuel P. Huntington's proposal that NATO adopt a "conventional retaliatory offensive strategy." His argument is that NATO should *promptly* attack into Eastern Europe as soon as Warsaw Pact units cross the border, rather than concentrate solely upon expelling enemy forces from NATO territory.[36] Huntington advocates going further than FOFA in attacking the second echelon by using ground forces to seize Warsaw Pact valued assets and East European territory. This has raised questions among American military planners:

---

[34] Josef Joffe, "Stability and Its Discontent: Should NATO Go Conventional?" *The Washington Quarterly,* Fall 1984, p. 136.

[35] See "Guerre: les Armes qui vont tout changer," *Le Nouvel Observateur,* November 2, 1984, p. 97.

[36] Samuel P. Huntington, "Conventional Deterrence and Conventional Retaliation In Europe," *International Security,* Winter 1983–84, pp. 32–56.

How would such escalation be controlled? How would such a conflict be terminated once it has been expanded? And if the Soviets are backed into their own corner, does this not risk lowering the nuclear threshold?[37] The strongest objections, however, have come from the West Europeans who not only see such a strategy as risky and dangerous, but who far prefer to reemphasize nuclear deterrence rather than encourage the spread of a high-intensity conventional conflict throughout all of Europe to the Soviet border.[38]

Scenarios for deep strike have been criticized as raising problems for crisis stability and political control. The decision to escalate by striking second- and third-echelon Warsaw Pact forces might have to be made at an early, and still ambiguous, stage of the conflict. The compression of decision-making time required for some of the proposed new technologies, such as ballistic missiles for use in counter-air roles, could reduce effective political control. The speed of military operations that emerging technologies and deep strike tactics would generate could, some argue, limit the flexibility of political leaders to make decisions and necessitate giving the military a freer rein. A disadvantage of a strategy that calls for rapid escalation in depth, therefore, is that it could result in "locking in" decisions that ought not be made until the situation at hand can be fully evaluated. Although there is some merit to this concern, it should, nonetheless, not be beyond the ability of NATO's political and military leadership through careful planning to safeguard against the loss of adequate political control.

Conclusions: On Future Policy

The present ferment over enhancing conventional defense can prove to be an important step toward a safer and more stable

---

[37]Keith A. Dunn and William O. Standenmaier, "The Retaliatory Offensive and Operational Realities in NATO," *Survival*, May/June 1985, pp. 108–118.

[38]See, for example, Eckhard Lübkemeier, *Deterrence, Détente and Defense in Europe: How Not to Reform NATO's Strategy*, Bonn: Friedrich Ebert Stiftung, May 1984.

East-West environment, as well as a more collaborative trans-Atlantic relationship, provided that it is carefully and constructively channeled. The risk is that it could exacerbate the military confrontation in Europe and sow greater discord within the Atlantic Alliance.

There are no magical, technical fixes to complex, political problems. As we have seen, there is still a wide range of uncertainties over the feasibility and fundability of emerging technologies as well as the desirability of some of the new military doctrines.

No doubt it is a good thing that much thought and attention is now being given to ways to reduce NATO's dependence upon the early-use of nuclear weapons. Yet we should recognize that there exists no European-American consensus on the extent to which the Alliance should move toward reliance on conventional arms—and such a consensus is unlikely to develop given the differing perspectives on the two sides of the Atlantic.

We should increase the range of flexibility within the strategy of flexible response. We should give SACEUR the means to provide conventional defense for weeks, rather than days, before a necessary recourse to nuclear weapons. Yet, the Western publics would be deluding themselves if they thought that measures of this sort would provide a way out of the nuclear dilemma in Europe. Even a "perfect" conventional balance between the two military blocs on the continent will not alter the need for a nuclear basis for Western Europe's security so long as there remains a Soviet nuclear threat.

Important improvements to the means of implementing flexible response are available and should be adopted where feasible. Apart from the proposals examined in this essay, there are others, such as those discussed especially in West Germany, that call for strategies of "non-provocative defense" or "territorial defense" based on the training and equipping of militia forces and large numbers of civilian reservists. Another would be a long overdue correction in the current maldeployment of national forces in West Germany, so as to have NATO forces more effectively positioned at the places of greatest military danger along the Iron Curtain. But we should be clear that for the indefinite future there is no valid alternative to the doctrine of flexible response. Neither a NATO strategy that is *all* conventional nor one that is *all* nuclear will receive a sufficient level of public support.

Emerging technologies should be adopted *selectively*. This is not the argument of the Luddite, opposed to any new technology. There is no reason why the NATO countries should deny themselves the advantage of their superior technological base. Two new technologies that could greatly improve NATO's combat effectiveness without creating doctrinal problems, for example, are the LANTIRN all-weather night attack capability for fighters and the AGM-130 air-guided munition, which can deliver cluster bombs at ranges of up to 30 kilometers. In a number of additional cases emerging technology will enhance military effectiveness and may serve to reduce the need for manpower or for reliance on nuclear weapons systems.

Decisions on the acquisition of specific emerging technologies should *not* be taken, however, solely on the basis of what is technologically feasible or available. Also to be considered should be the consequences of the choice of the weapon system for other factors, such as crisis stability or the nature of the Soviet response. This should certainly be the case for the Anti-Tactical Ballistic Missile (ATBM) system for defense against short-range Soviet missiles that is currently being proposed as a "European SDI." There was, therefore, a great deal of merit in Manfred Wörner's call for a "conceptual military framework" that takes into account political and economic, as well as military, considerations in assessing emerging technologies and in adopting new military strategies. The Alliance's recent efforts toward developing such a framework are to be commended, although its assignment to NATO's Military Committee may have limited the scope of the undertaking.

The primary impediment to improving conventional defense will be resource constraints. This is especially the case for emerging technologies for deep strike roles. Not only will their sophistication make them expensive, but in many cases they will have weapons missions that will supplement existing military roles rather than substitute for them.

Political leaders must be realistic in assessing the prospects for funding the costs of enhanced conventional defense. A case can be made that without the four percent that the Rogers Plan calls for there will, in fact, be a net reduction in NATO's present capabilities. And yet it appears unlikely that the Alliance will even extend the largely unmet three percent goal beyond its currently planned termination in 1986.

The real problem that the Alliance could face for the rest of this decade may be how to prevent a *decline* in its conventional efforts rather than how to enhance them. The estimated cost of a package that would include improving NATO's defense in depth *plus* emerging technologies and deep strike is seven percent annual real growth. Because of the slow growth of the European and American economies, and a variety of additional economic, social welfare and other factors, including competing defense goals, there is extremely little prospect that parliaments and publics will support a conventional force improvement of this size.

What is essential, therefore, is that the Alliance develop a clear sense of its own priorities. The various initiatives and proposals of the past two or three years have created some confusion in this regard. The first priority must remain the defense of Western Europe against an initial Warsaw Pact attack at or near the border. This means adequate funding for infrastructure, war stocks, aircraft shelters, protection of communications, and whatever else is needed to provide for the readiness and sustainability of NATO's forces. It makes little sense to spend money on the deep attack of the Warsaw Pact second and third echelons if as a result NATO loses the ability to contain the initial attack across the border. Of course, not all such choices are clear zero-sum situations. Nevertheless, a maximum delay in the recourse to the use of nuclear weapons is essential.

There are, in addition, other tradeoffs within national defense programs that ought to be weighed by political leaders, although they seldom are in a systematic manner. For example, might not spending on conventional defense in Europe be a better investment for war-avoidance and national security than 50 MX missiles or two new aircraft carriers for the United States, or Trident submarines for Great Britain, or the Force d'Action Rapide for France? Such questions can only be addressed in the context of broad and informed national debates; and the answer will only be in the affirmative if the non-nuclear defense of Western Europe is clearly recognized as being close to the top in priority.

With the fiscal pressure on defense budgets increasing and the costs of conventional arms growing exponentially, there is a clear necessity to improve the weapons acquisition and modernization process on an Alliance-wide basis. Emerging technologies provide an excellent opportunity to move in this direction, perhaps through the creation of a new mechanism for coordinating research and development on new technologies and allocating production to different nations. One hesitates three times before suggesting another institutional arrangement although, in fact, nothing intended for this purpose exists at present. Nevertheless, the pooling of technological know-how and research and development efforts may be essential if expensive, unaffordable duplication is to be minimized.

The United States has a special responsibility in this regard. The trans-Atlantic imbalance in arms procurement favors the United States by between three-to-one and seven-to-one depending upon the figures used, according to David M. Abshire, the current U.S. Ambassador to NATO.[39] The chorus of complaints in Europe about the unequal traffic on the two-way street is not without justification even though there was some improvement during 1985. Emerging technologies within new weapons systems provide the chance to improve this imbalance in a coherent, planned manner. Despite the formidable political, economic and military pressures to maintain independent, national defense industrial capabilities, the Europeans are making some progress in coordinating and rationalizing their efforts through the IEPG. This now needs to be expanded into, or connected with, a European-American arrangement, be it accomplished through a new institutional arrangement or just informally. Above all, the United States needs to acquire a better appreciation of the fact that its political and security interests will

---

[39]See "New Technology and Intra-Alliance Relationships: New Strengths, New Strains" in *New Technology and Western Security Policy*, London: International Institute for Strategic Studies, Adelphi Paper No. 199, Part III, Summer 1985, p. 12.

be well served in the long run by the maintenance in Western Europe of viable defense industries and a healthy technological base—even if it means self-denial on a few lucrative sales.

The potential impact on arms control of ET and deep strike is far from clear but careful consideration should be given before deploying new systems that could impair the reaching of arms control agreements in the Mutual and Balanced Force Reduction negotiations or other forums. "Dual capable" systems, for example, can greatly complicate the verification of arms control accords. Objections have been raised about the deployment of conventionally armed ballistic missiles on the grounds that the Soviets would have difficulty in distinguishing between a nonnuclear and a nuclear-tipped incoming missile. Such a missile, if targeted upon Warsaw Pact command posts could, it is argued, induce the Soviets to preempt by launching their nuclear weapons before the NATO missile reaches its target. Of course, such a Soviet preemptive response would be irrational if it should commence a nuclear war. It is also the case that substantial ambiguity already exists in Central Europe with regard to dual capable systems. The Soviet SS–21 and SS–23 surface-to-surface missiles can deliver either nuclear or conventional warheads, as can some of NATO's manned aircraft. Nevertheless, the complication that new technologies can create for arms control could become a growing political issue within the Alliance if not astutely handled. Several West European governments, for example, have already indicated they would not allow dual capable ballistic missiles to be based on their soil.

This leads to the final point. Although the renewed attention being given to conventional defense is to be welcomed, it could also lead to a deeply divisive debate. The doctrinal differences remain significant and, in a climate of technological competition combined with resource constraints, there will be ample opportunity for accusations and recriminations. There are other major items on the current agenda of the Atlantic Alliance, such as the Strategic Defense Initiative, the growing imbalance between Europe and America in advanced civilian technology, and serious differences over trade policy that could grow as sources of friction. All these issues are interrelated not only in the economics—funding for SDI and ET may be in direct competition with one another—but in the politics of the Alliance. In considering new measures to improve conventional defense, it will be essential that political leaders take into account the political strains and stresses within the trans-Atlantic system as a whole.

Richard D. DeLauer

Emerging Technologies and their Impact on the Conventional Deterrent

In light of both the numerical superiority of the Warsaw Pact forces and the evident deficiencies in the NATO conventional warfare capability that exist today, it is imperative that the Alliance reexamine the structural makeup of its forces as well as the assigned roles and missions of its land and air forces. Such a reexamination is urgently needed and should include a thorough consideration of the potential offered by the West's present advantage in advanced technology. In my view, an objective reexamination based on this premise will show that a significantly enhanced conventional deterrent is achievable and can be implemented within the next decade with a commitment of resources only slightly greater than that now being contemplated by the Alliance nations.

The conventional arms force structure of the NATO membernations has for many years been predicated on the traditional concepts of post-World War II warfare. NATO land forces rely on a doctrine of active defense, and their combat style is based on attrition of combat forces and resources. The NATO tactical air forces consist primarily of high performance, manned aircraft armed with weapons that favor air-to-air combat. In recent years, the U.S. Navy has emphasized forward force projection centered on the aircraft carrier battle group and the nuclear attack submarine, while the European navies have focused on sealane control along with making some effort to maintain coastal control.

To counter these conventional warfare concepts and doctrine, the Warsaw Pact has based its land and air force structure on a strategy of numerical superiority. It plans to employ these superior forces using a tactical doctrine that relies on a massive initial surprise assault by a large number of mobile land units deployed simultaneously on multiple fronts. This is to be followed closely by rapid reinforcement of the first-echelon troops from rear staging areas. In addition, the Warsaw Pact doctrine calls for combined air and airborne operations to achieve suppression of NATO's air defense capabilities as well as rear-echelon interdiction.

The modifications to the structure of NATO land forces that now need to be made should selectively enhance their survivability against a surprise, multipronged, combined arms attack by numerically superior Warsaw Pact forces. These modifications would include such things as enhanced self-defense capabilities for NATO air-to-surface systems, greater use of forward sensors, and the rapid fusion of sensor data to provide near "real-time" battlefield management data to NATO commanders. In addition, tactical concepts that exploit the recent experience gained in the Middle East in defending versus attacking urban areas should be adopted. For NATO air forces, changes should be introduced both in the platform configurations and in mission tactics. When undertaken, such changes would permit NATO forces to carry out a more effective attack on the Warsaw Pact follow-on forces.

Since the Soviet doctrine calls for the rapid reinforcement of the forward line of troops (FLOT) from second and follow-on echelons deployed to the rear, the need to attack and disrupt these rear echelons has been designated by NATO as the mission of "Follow-on Forces Attack" (FOFA). This concept requires the implementation of a deep strike capability for the NATO land forces to penetrate a considerable distance (e.g., 20 to 60 km) behind the FLOT and for the NATO air forces to carry out coordinated attacks to interdict the Warsaw Pact rear-echelon land forces and supply depots as well as to deliver heavy attacks on the Warsaw Pact tactical air bases and surface-to- surface tactical missile installations.

Another reason for considering such changes in doctrine at this time results from new doctrine that is now being implemented by the U.S. Army on a worldwide basis, one that has been designated "Airland Battle." This doctrine, instituted in

1982, represents a major shift in battle strategy and tactics. In brief, it assigns primary battle management responsibility to the corps commander instead of to the division commanders, focusing the land battle operations at the corps level instead of at the tactical level of the division as in the previous doctrine of "Active Defense." The combat style in the Airland Battle doctrine is one of maneuver rather than attrition and involves a balance between defense and offense, instead of pure defense as was the orientation in the Active Defense doctrine.

Finally, an American concept referred to as "Counter-Air 90" is being discussed seriously in NATO at this time. In its present form, Counter-Air 90 is based on upgrading all the major NATO counter air assets; better self-defense for NATO surface-to-air systems against tactical ballistic missile attack—in fact, an antitactical ballistic missile (ATBM) capability; and greater emphasis on a capability to attack Warsaw Pact tactical air bases with a multiple set of systems, including surface-to-surface conventional warhead ballistic missiles, standoff air-launched missiles, and defense suppression by remotely piloted vehicles (RPV). The airfield attack capability must consist not only of runway cratering munitions—which have only limited effectiveness as a means of disrupting tactical air operations—but also should include the capability to attack and destroy the servicing and rearming facilities as well as the sheltered aircraft themselves.

In all of these new concepts and doctrines, the common need is for the rapid acquisition and dissemination of targeting and intelligence data, for highly accurate weapons guidance systems, and for highly effective munitions. These requirements must be coupled with the provision of more survivable delivery systems. The reason that such capabilities and warfare concepts are now being considered seriously by the Alliance results in large measure from the rapid advances being made in the West in the necessary technologies.

The new technologies have been loosely referred to as "emerging technologies." They have now reached the point where their insertion into the military inventory of the NATO forces is readily at hand. It is only by the vigorous pursuit of these technologies and the related advanced warfare concepts that the Alliance can expect to overcome the vast numerical superiority enjoyed by the Warsaw Pact forces. If this can be accomplished, the survivability and effectiveness of NATO forces could be enhanced to the point where our NATO commanders would essentially be relieved of the present need to rely on the early-use of theater nuclear weapons to counter a massive Warsaw Pact conventional arms attack.

Without question, any available options that would delay the employment of tactical nuclear weapons in response to a conventional attack should be a highly desirable objective for the nations of the Western Alliance.

Unfortunately, the debate has focused for the past several years on the issue of the modernization of the Atlantic Alliance's nuclear forces, particularly the status of theater nuclear forces. Intensive Soviet political activities in the 1981–1983 time frame were aimed at altering NATO's plans to base the Pershing II intermediate-range nuclear missile and the ground-launched cruise missile (GLCM) in several of the member-nations of the Alliance. There was an emotional debate on the issue and many partisan demonstrations took place before the respective governments eventually secured parliamentary approval to accommodate the basing of these improved-capability theater nuclear weapons.

In contrast, the question of the shortcomings of the Alliance's conventional force structure has not enjoyed the same level of comment except from some professionals. The Conference of National Armaments Directors and the Military Committee of NATO carried out studies, analyses and evaluations of the adequacy of the conventional force and its composition for more than three years without reaching significant agreement on a future course of action.

Perhaps a part of the reason for this indecision was the fact that at the higher levels of government the consideration of defense issues was almost always focused on the amount of national funding to be committed to the military forces rather than on strategic concepts and missions. Annual budget increases of two percent or three percent after inflation (whatever that was interpreted to mean) were argued on both sides of the Atlantic, but little consideration was given to just what the money was to be spent on. The United States, however, regularly urged the

Europeans to accept the notion that their exploitation of certain emerging technologies was the most effective way to utilize additional resources. These efforts included formal proposals by the U.S. Secretary of Defense and detailed suggestions by his subordinates at almost every available NATO forum. The argument has been that a vigorously pursued program to improve conventional armaments through new technology would result in a military advantage that would offset the Warsaw Pact's numerical superiority. The United States has kept up this steady drumbeat because it has been clearly apparent for some time that the NATO conventional force structure was inadequate and completely unable to cope militarily with the forces being maintained in forward areas by the Warsaw Pact.

In oversimplified terms, these emerging technologies are expected to enable the military commander to have rapid access to information from a multiple set of sensors, from which the data are fused and analyzed and represented in the format needed for effective command decisions. The commander in the field will be able to select from among various responses available to him for use. If the response calls for the delivery of munitions by airborne platforms, the delivery will be "stealthy"—that is, essentially invisible to most radar and defensive fire control systems. These munitions will also possess "smart" weapon terminal guidance capabilities that could produce target accuracies within only a few meters.

The Threat

The Soviet Union favors means other than direct military aggression to pursue its objectives vis-à-vis the nations of the Atlantic Alliance. Thus, the U.S.S.R. uses its extensive military capability as an instrument of coercion and political manipulation to serve its aims and interests. The strategy of NATO on the other hand, is to deter aggression and to frustrate Soviet aims by means short of war. For NATO to present a credible deterrent to Soviet military threats, however, it must maintain a strong military force in being and on call, in terms of both conventional warfare and in terms of tactical and strategic nuclear weapons. The latter are held in reserve as a threat so that a conventional attack could be escalated flexibly to a tactical or theater nuclear conflict if conditions warrant.

But NATO's strategy is defensive. The Alliance will not initiate a war and will only engage in defensive combat if it cannot be avoided. To be able to avoid hostilities, NATO must maintain strong and verifiable defensive military forces in Central Europe sufficient to discourage the Warsaw Pact forces from considering aggression as a viable option. NATO must also maintain a strong enough military presence in Europe to reassure the people of the Atlantic Alliance that it has an effective deterrent. This deterrent must be structured and deployed in a way that is convincing and credible, both to the Soviets and also to the Alliance nations.

In the event that the Soviet Union should be tempted to mount an attack on the NATO forces in Western Europe, the current Soviet strategy and operational concept calls for a concentrated ground and air assault aimed at achieving overwhelming victory in the shortest possible time. Opposing the NATO forces is an impressive array of Soviet and non-Soviet Warsaw Pact men and machines capable of mounting a massive non-nuclear attack on a very broad front in Central Europe.

Comparing the Soviet/Warsaw Pact forces stationed in Eastern Europe with the NATO forces on active duty or rapidly deployable in Western Europe, the Soviets, according to the most recent U.S. Department of Defense estimates currently have a numerical advantage of about 1.5 to 1 in total military personnel; better than 2 to 1 in main battle tanks; 1.6 to 1 in armored personnel carriers/fighting vehicles; at least 1.6 to 1 in artillery, anti-tank weapons, and mortars; and 2 to 1 in attack helicopters.[1] They also possess significant numbers of modernized tactical ballistic missiles, the SS–21, SS–22, and SS–23, capable of delivering payloads that may contain conventional explosives, chemical/biological agents, or nuclear warheads.

In spite of this quantitative advantage, the Soviet strategy and operational concept is based on three principal elements: (1) sur-

---

[1] *Soviet Military Power 1985*, 4th edition, Washington D.C.: Government Printing Office, 1985.

prise at both the strategic and tactical levels in order to catch the NATO forces before they can achieve mobilization and full deployment; (2) an integrated combined arms offensive, employing air power and surface-to-surface missiles, forward deployed ground forces to press the initial attack, and reserve echelons of follow-on forces to exploit the offensive; and (3) combat momentum achieved with superior numerical forces, concentrated firepower, and highly mobile and maneuverable operations. Soviet use of nuclear arms rather than reliance on its conventional arms concept is felt to be unlikely, since the Soviets are believed to be well aware of the ever-present threat of instant nuclear retaliation by NATO, not only in the theater of conflict, but also against the Soviet homeland if such an attack were undertaken against the NATO defenders.

In addition to the element of surprise, current Soviet offensive concepts for the initial attack also involve the dispersion of their attacks on a large number of axes of advance; high speed and momentum in order to press and sustain the initial assault; the use of massive helicopter assaults and intensive artillery bombardments to suppress and disrupt the defensive buildup; and the use of special maneuvering groups employing helicopter transport as well as high-mobility armored units to reach key points in the defender's rear areas in order to destroy the cohesion of the NATO defensive forces at the outset.

Although the Soviet doctrine obviously is well conceived and presents a formidable threat to the Alliance, its success is not automatically guaranteed, and the Soviets understandably have some serious uncertainties about their ability to achieve their intended degree of strategic and tactical surprise. They also have substantial concerns regarding the adequacy of their largely untested concepts and forces, the extent to which their lower levels of command are capable of flexibility and initiative of tactical operations, the extent to which their Warsaw Pact allies can be relied upon to implement the operational scheme, and the ever-present threat of a rapid escalation of the conflict through exercise of the nuclear option by the NATO command.

Additionally, the Soviet high command recognizes certain vulnerable aspects in its attack doctrine, including the necessity for a very rapid and complete victory over the NATO forces, the highly rigid and preplanned nature of the Soviet offensive doctrine, the U.S.S.R.'s critical dependence on (ever-lengthening) lines of supply for an uninterrupted flow of follow-on forces to press the attack, the need for effective command and control to realize the full impact of the integrated combined arms offensive, the critical need for effective and flexible lines of communication, and the need for a very high concentration of forces, which renders them extremely vulnerable to NATO conventional and nuclear response.

Responses to the Threat

In order to understand where technological improvements in the conventional warfare capabilities of Alliance forces might contribute to the containment and defeat of such formidable opposition, we should first review the details of present NATO strategy. It is one of deterrence, both by maintaining sufficiently strong conventional forces to discourage the Soviets from attempting an attack because their military assessment indicates it would be either unsuccessful or excessively costly, and by reason of their understanding that such an attack would trigger a massive and punishing response on their deployed forces and potentially on their rear areas and the Soviet homeland itself. Such a punitive response is recognized by the Soviets to be conventional at the outset, but the threat of rapid escalation to nuclear weapons is also seen to be a part of the NATO doctrine.

The NATO deterrent concept is based on maintaining an ability to blunt the initial Soviet ground/air attack on Western Europe and then on holding the forward positions of the engaged NATO forces until they can be reinforced through the rapid mobilization and deployment of reserve forces and supporting matériel from both sides of the Atlantic to the European battlefront. This concept is, in my opinion, recognized to be unrealistic at the present time, particularly in light of the overwhelming superiority of the opposing Soviet/Warsaw Pact forces and the very limited extent of propositioned Alliance munitions and support assets in Europe.

In reality, NATO's defense concept is based on the *early-use* of nuclear weapons to counter any major Warsaw Pact attack.

Within a very few days of the start of any Soviet advance into Western European territory, the Supreme Allied Commander Europe would be forced to request permission for the utilization of nuclear weapons, initially limited-range theater nuclear weapons. However, there is always the potential of escalation to longer range weapons if the situation demands it. While this concept based on nuclear deterrence has served the Alliance effectively for the past several decades, the political realities of the future may force a change toward less reliance on the nuclear element. The degree of political unrest that resulted from the Soviet's intensive propaganda campaign against the recent deployment of the modernized Pershing II surface-to-surface ballistic missiles and of the GLCM in several Alliance countries may well be just a forerunner of the future. With such a possibility in the offing, what can be done by the members of the Alliance to counter it?

Let us examine briefly the requirements of deterrence. For a deterrent to be considered viable, it must have the following characteristics. First, it must consist of a military capability that is survivable against any realistic threat that it is posed against. Second, it must be recognized as having the potential to be effective when it is employed. Finally, it must be perceived by the opposition that there is the political will to employ it. These characteristics are necessary for either strategic (nuclear) or nonstrategic (conventional) deterrence.

The strategic nuclear deterrent efforts of the Alliance have been focused on one or the other of these elements for the past decade. In the United States, the major arguments have been over the land-based and air-breathing legs of the strategic triad. There is no fundamental disagreement that the MX represents a major increase in strategic nuclear effectiveness. The question has been whether or not the missile could be provided with an operational basing mode that would assure the survivability of the force in the event of a Soviet offensive attack on the United States.

The problem with the U.S. strategic manned bomber force was similar in nature. Here, the issue was that the B-52 force was not survivable, either on the ground or enroute because of the Soviet submarine-launched ballistic missile threat, their air-to-air superiority, and their surface-to-air terminal defenses. Although the development of the long-range, air-launched cruise missile provides standoff capability that mitigates terminal defenses, it did little for the base escape and enroute survivability problems. The modernization of the U.S. manned strategic bomber fleet by the B–1 and the Advanced Technology Bomber is needed to overcome these weaknesses.

With regard to the will to utilize these strategic forces, there is no question that the present incumbent in the White House is indeed seen as having such will. Therefore, the U.S. modernized nuclear forces do in fact constitute a credible strategic deterrent to a Soviet attack. How much longer this state of affairs can be expected to continue is difficult to forecast. Certainly, in one form or another, the strategic nuclear deterrent has retained its effectiveness in behalf of the United States and its NATO allies for over 40 years. Therefore, it can realistically be expected to continue for the foreseeable future.

However, with respect to NATO strategy for a war in Europe, it is not as clear that the Europeans have sufficient political will to continue to support a nuclear-based defensive concept without some real progress in the arms control arena, particularly if the Soviet propaganda campaign continues unabated. Therefore, the possibility of a NATO doctrine that is not based on the early utilization of nuclear weapons, but rather on improved conventional weapons capabilities should be examined. Such an examination must be undertaken with the understanding that in order to be truly credible, a deterrent must be survivable, it must be effective, and there must be a genuine will to use it.

How is this to be accomplished? First, a realistic assessment of the threat must be agreed to and accepted by the Alliance. Second, the threat must be met by exploiting the West's strength, which is its leadership in advanced technology. This should include the sharing of technology and rationalization of research and development throughout the Alliance. We must insure that there is authentic political support for such a technology improvement program, including a willingness to make the necessary investments over a considerable period of time. Third, the present military concepts and doctrine must be critically reexamined and definitions of roles and missions must be revised where necessary. This will be the most difficult task. Strong arguments against change will be presented by entrenched constituents. But the payoff can be so dramatic that every effort must be made to try to make such an initiative a reality.

Emerging Technologies

In recent years much has been said about the emerging technologies—or to be more precise, the emerg*ed* and the emerg*ing* technologies. However, it is only now that they have reached the level of development where serious consideration should be given to the concepts and doctrine that would effectively utilize their advantages.

What are these technologies? They are hardware and software that can accomplish a rapid assimilation of intelligence and operational data from many independent sources and sensors. They can quickly—essentially with the speed of light—analyze these data, select the necessary battle management option and present it to field commanders in a form that will permit the most effective decision for retaliation. The weapons will be carried on low-observable platforms, which are not detectable by radar, and will attack the enemy with munitions that are highly effective against his mobile forces and accurate within a few meters. Such a response will result in high attrition of the attacker's forces and high survivability for the defender. If the degree of attrition is unacceptable to the attacker he will be deterred from pressing such an attack.

By judiciously using the emerging technologies, we can improve the capability of NATO forces to acquire distant targets; obtain surveillance and intelligence information; improve the communication between remote sensors, command centers, and weapons; utilize advanced methods for data fusion to consolidate, analyze, and disseminate battlefield status and intelligence information; increase the effectiveness of combined air and land anti-air, anti-armor and counterbattery tactics; and enhance the capability to interdict enemy rear areas through remote target acquisition, standoff weapons attack, and long-range attack on enemy reserve forces, resupply areas, airfields and depots.

Typical emerging technologies that can be effectively integrated with existing and new weapons systems to fulfill these objectives include, among others, very high speed integrated circuits (VHSIC), low observable (Stealth) technology, advanced software/algorithm technology, fail soft/fault tolerant electronics, artificial intelligence, very high speed ("super") computers, advanced materials and composites, high density monolithic focal place arrays, fiber optics, high-energy lasers, anti-jam communications and precise navigation systems, and real-time data fusion and battle management systems.

Incorporating these kinds of emerging technologies into conventional military systems and equipment would provide the Alliance with an enhanced capability by making available such improved weapons systems as small CEP (circular error probability) conventional area weapons; modular families of wideband, anti-jam communications; near real-time data correlation systems for battlefield command and control; near-zero CEP standoff weapons; robust loiter weapons; robust long-range sensors and decoys; advanced electronic warfare systems; and low-cost, anti-jam, very precise navigation systems.

The U.S. Department of Defense Emerging Technology Initiative (ET) includes technologies and programs that are broader in scope than those needed to accomplish the FOFA mission. Some programs such as the terminally guided submissiles for the Multiple Launch Rocket System (MLRS) that are included in the close-in battle program are as technically challenging as those included in the longer range attack set for the deep strike mission. However, since these deep battle programs, being pursued jointly by the Army and Air Force, are the most challenging from the military operation and policy perspectives, much attention has been paid to them.

The United States, like its NATO allies, has stressed standoff surveillance and targeting at the expense of penetrating unmanned systems. This is the result of an emphasis by the United States on real-time systems that could serve the dual purpose of providing intelligence and warning before the onset of hostilities, as well as strike data during wartime. The United States is emphasizing three systems to provide this standoff capability, with two of the three nearing operational deployment. The Precision Location Strike System (PLSS) is a sensor capable of accurately locating enemy targets, primarily associated with the Soviet air defense system. The Advanced Synthetic Aperture Radar System (ASARS) is a high-quality, all-weather, imaging radar capable of high accuracy location and classification of stationary tactical targets. Both systems are completing development and beginning deployment for use on the TR-1 reconnaissance aircraft. These sensors, which are already in the European theater, have been sufficiently tested in operational environments to give field commanders confidence that targets for deep strike can be found and classified. A contract for the third sensor system, the Joint Surveillance and Target Attack Radar System (JSTARS), was signed recently and European field trials and deployment are scheduled before the end of this decade. As these advanced sensor systems mature, the United States will move toward acquiring unmanned drones as complements to these standoff systems. At present, however, both the operational concepts and equipment maturity are severely lagging for these types of unmanned systems.

Computer-based battle management systems offer the ability to combine theater intelligence and targeting sensor data into an integrated picture of the battlefield and distribute it to the tactical field commanders for assessment and strike execution. Several first-generation systems based on mini-computers have been deployed with U.S. forces in Europe and elsewhere. The Limited Operational Capability Europe (LOCE) and Target Analysis and Planning System (TAPS) are examples. These systems are being used by U.S. forces to develop and refine procedures for the FOFA mission with strike assets already on hand in the theater. At the present time, it appears to be very likely that the next generation equipment such as the Joint Tactical Fusion Program (JTFP) and the Joint Tactical Information Distribution System (JTIDS) will be deployed to a force prepared to accept them. Both of these systems are well along in the development cycle, and initial deployments are expected in the next few years.

The least mature of the emerging technology developments are the weapons. Deep strike weapons for deployment by ground forces from the MLRS launcher or from aircraft are currently in development for deployment before the end of the decade. Typical targets are airfields, enemy systems such as air defense sites and command, control and communications facilities, and mobile armor columns. Delivery means include both ballistic and cruise missiles as well as aircraft-delivered dispensers. A typical operational approach might involve a missile attack on enemy airfields to suppress Warsaw Pact air sorties while aircraft-delivered and standoff weapons suppress enemy air defenses in order to support penetrating air strikes against important land targets. While these defense suppression and counter-air campaigns are under way, complementary standoff missile attacks against ground targets such as enemy armor columns would be undertaken.

Although the development risk for these advanced technology weapons is comparatively higher than for the sensor and battle management systems, the United States has concentrated on the need for a variety of warheads and delivery means in order to distribute the risk. Delivery means progressing from simple dispensers to long-range ballistic and cruise missiles are currently under development. Warheads progressing from dumb bomblets through runway penetrators, emitter homers, and smart anti-armor homing submunitions are also under development or already in production.

In April 1984 the NATO Conference of National Armaments Directors drew up a list of candidate projects for inclusion in an initial emerging technologies application program designed for operational deployment within the next ten years. In approximate decreasing order of priority, this list included the following projects:

- NATO Identification System (Identification, Friend or Foe);*
- Electronic warfare systems for helicopters;
- Electronic jamming systems for tactical aircraft;
- Standoff radar surveillance and target acquisition system (based on or similar to the U.S. JSTARS);
- Ground-based electronic support system to process sensor data;*
- Short-range anti-radiation missile (SRAM);*
- Low-cost powered dispenser for use against fixed targets;

54 / The Conventional Defense of Europe

- Terminally guided warhead (TGW) for the MLRS*;
- Medium-range RPV for battlefield surveillance and target acquisition;*
- Autonomous precision-guided munitions for 155 mm artillery;
- Artillery locating system (counterbattery radar).

If we pursue these and related emerging technologies with diligence, it is possible that within the next decade NATO could field a very muchy more effective and survivable conventional military force—one that could be every bit as effective and successful as the present nuclear deterrent has been for the past 40 years.

What Needs to Be Changed?

Much has to be changed from the present situation if we are to be successful in creating a significantly improved conventional deterrent. Take for instance the question of survivability of our tactical forces; much has to be done to improve the mobility and the self-defense capability of these forces. As mentioned previously, Soviet tactical air resources, the increased accuracy of the SS–21 and SS–23 surface-to-surface missile systems, as well as the increased range of the SS–23s make it imperative that something be done about the self-defense of our anti-air capacity.

This self-protection capability should include ATBM systems capable of countering Soviet tactical ballistic missiles such as the SS–21, SS–22, and SS–23. At the present time, the NATO surface-to-air defense systems—the Patriot, the Roland, the Hawk, the Rapier—while mobile, are not mobile to the extent required for survivability and are extremely soft considering the range, payload and accuracy of Soviet surface-to-surface and air-to-surface tactical missiles. This must be changed. Our surface-to-air defensive capabilities must be made as mobile as possible, and in addition, they must be modified so as to provide some self-protection capability—including an ATBM capability.

---

*Projects deemed necessary (but not sufficient) to implement FOFA, Deep Strike, Airland Battle, Counter-Air 90, etc.

To reduce attrition of our manned aircraft, RPVs for both passive surveillance and defense suppression must be utilized extensively. They are developed and, in fact, were combat-proven by the Israelis in the Lebanon invasions, yet the Alliance has very few operational RPVs in service. Why? Because it would require a major change in the doctrine that now exists—not only within the Alliance, but in the national military organizations of the Alliance, particularly of the United States.

Present roles and missions do not lend themselves easily to the concept of a highly integrated land and air battle management doctrine. In the case of non-piloted aircraft, who is to own them, who is to control them, and, most important, which service is to allocate the necessary resources to the acquisition and operation of these weapons? These resources must be reallocated from those already devoted to existing systems. In the case of the Air Force, perhaps a reduction in the number of manned aircraft will be necessary. For the Army, it may require a reduction in combat infantry units, tanks, artillery, or armored fighting vehicles. Much of the present thinking must be modified and compromises made. Resources must also be spent on interoperability, particularly of the NATO command, control and communications capability.

An encouraging development in this area has been the recent agreements between the Chiefs of Staff of the U.S. Army and of the U.S. Air Force. A memorandum of understanding defining the role of each service in the Airland Battle has been agreed upon. Whether this positive step forward will continue beyond their respective tours of duty remains to be seen.

In addition to these decisions on force mix, changing the current situation requires the diverting of resources from presently deployed platforms and weapons into something new and something different. However, this is the only way that we are going to be able to solve the dilemma that we face—the dilemma of an enemy who has a greater numbers of assets deployed and who devotes at least three to seven times as much of his gross national product to maintaining these advantages as do the combined nations of the Alliance.[2] The consequence of this is obvious: the Alliance will never gain numerical parity with the opposed Soviet/Warsaw Pact forces, therefore the West must make its inferior numbers of men and equipment more survivable and more effective.

To take the question of survivability as an example, U.S. tactical aircraft stationed in Western Europe have a very low potential for survivability if a concentrated Soviet attack takes place. Until recently, at least, about 50 percent of the U.S. tactical aircraft were housed in shelters that had a reasonable degree of hardness, but almost none of the European aircraft were. This situation is currently being improved. Although the Alliance has a tremendous number of runways available to them for dispersion, which provides an opportunity for increasing survivability, these airfields do not have servicing and rearming capabilities that are sheltered. Thus, all reservicing and rearming must be done in soft conditions. It seems ironic that with shelters costing only about $1 million each, the procurement of one less $30 million airplane would permit the shelter of 30 additional $30 million aircraft. Yet it was only in the last two years that the U.S. Air Force made this obviously advantageous tradeoff.

The situation must be further improved. While we have the ability to provide a certain amount of self-defense capability to existing surface-to-air units, a more effective way to increase the

---

[2] My estimates differ from most official (i.e., CIA) numbers because the CIA model does not count anything until it is observed by intelligence resources. My numbers take into account such "invisible" items as plant modernization, investments in R&D, new prototypes, etc., which the CIA figures do not include. Moreover, I include a significant amount of resources and effort that come from what we call the civilian economy but that goes into the Soviet military security complex: such expenditures as the construction of tunnels from Moscow 60 km in two directions to give underground access to the High Level Command Posts. If we were to do this in the United States, it would appear as a line item in the Defense Department budget, but this is not the case with the Soviets.

survivability of our aircraft would be to provide considerably greater mobility to the aircraft themselves. The Alliance has not embraced vertical takeoff or short takeoff and landing technology to the degree that it could and should. U.S. tactical aircraft as well as the NATO tactical aircraft other than the Harrier or the U.S. Marine Corps AV–8B do not exploit short takeoff and landing or vertical takeoff and landing (VSTOL) to any degree. Also, we have the technology that could, at one stroke, make obsolescent most of the Soviet ground-based air surveillance and fire control systems and all their radar-guided missiles. This Stealth technology permits airborne platforms to present a very low radar signature. Neither the VSTOL nor Stealth technical solutions are being pursued in an aggressive fashion since, in both cases, their implementation would require that the aircraft compromise certain of their air-to-air dogfighting superiority.

While the foregoing discussion has largely concentrated on issues relating to the survivability of our existing air defense and tactical aircraft systems, there are also some important points to consider with respect to the contributions the emerged or emerging technologies can make to other elements of our forces. All of these are directly applicable to the conventional force capabilities needed to satisfy the NATO long-range goals of implementing the FOFA concept as well as for increasing and upgrading the effectiveness of our land and air forces in order ultimately to realize the doctrine of the Airland Battle.

The most important element of the allied command structure to be upgraded is the NATO integrated command, control, communications and intelligence (C^3I) capability. Progress is being made in this area, but at a pace that is much too slow. Since a substantial portion of the NATO C^3I infrastructure consists of the domestic telephone systems of the Alliance member-nations, improvements have in many instances been dependent upon political and economic decisions made by national ministries separate from their defense ministries. A case in point is the recent debate over whether or not to make the complete NATO communications system digital. West Germany was very slow to adopt a domestic digital telephone system, largely because of non-defense pressures, while the telephone systems of the United States and most of its allies were for the most part digital.

This has changed and now significant improvements can be made in the NATO communications net, including the installation of anti-jamming and secure voice features. When all these improvements have been fully implemented, the overall C^3I system capability will be greatly enhanced. These features are the result of advances in microelectronics and high speed data processing, which are included in the emerged technologies now available to all the members of the Alliance. In order to take complete advantage of the new technology, the participating members of the Alliance must expend the resources needed to acquire this improved capability.

Another conventional warfare area that could benefit from the emerged and emerging technologies is that of electronic warfare (EW). As previously mentioned, the Warsaw Pact forces operate in a very disciplined and structured fashion. Their operational concepts do not allow for very much flexibility or local initiative by the tactical commanders. Therefore, by disrupting their communications networks and offensive fire control systems, their numerical advantage can be considerably neutralized. The Alliance nations are extremely advanced in the technologies of EW. Many of the EW concepts and equipment developed by the West have been employed with great success by the Israelis in recent years. The problem is that NATO just does not possess enough of these sophisticated assets. Since the countermeasures competition is a continuing one, the Alliance needs constantly to develop and provide counter-countermeasure changes. This will require the expenditure of already limited resources and, like some other possible high leverage improvements to the NATO conventional warfare capability (e.g., Stealth, VSTOL), EW does not enjoy the priority it almost certainly deserves. Comments are offered below regarding the ability of the Alliance to improve its EW capabilities. Again, this is an area that depends heavily on advanced microelectronics technology, in which the West has a decided lead over the Warsaw Pact.

Although not directly dependent on the emerging technologies for improvement, another important area where the Alliance is extremely weak at present is that of chemical and biological warfare. The present situation is extremely dangerous: the Alliance is not capable of providing effective protection for its forces in the event of CW attack, let alone able to present a deterrent capability. The Soviets have extensive CW capabilities in place, and all their tactical surface-to-surface missiles are configured to carry CW payloads. They also equip their troops with modern protective equipment and conduct extensive training exercises under very realistic simulated CW conditions.

Even though our posture on CW is not dependent to any significant extent on advanced technology, it is in serious need of modernization through the application of existing and available technology. One aspect of chemical warfare, however, is closely related to the realization of the FOFA concept in which emerging technologies must play a definite role. When we have developed advanced systems for deep interdiction, the FOFA capability can be substantially enhanced if we provide an ability to deliver chemical munitions to enemy rear-area airfields. Such a capability would effectively disrupt Warsaw Pact tactical air operations and would also cause much of its reserve-echelon equipment to become unusable if not inoperable. Jet aircraft engines, ground and airborne radar systems, and other such sophisticated equipment can be effectively neutralized by the delivery of some relatively simple nonlethal chemicals, such as boron, certain acids, and carbon fibers. We should not continue to neglect these possibilities; the Soviets have not.

Technology Transfer

If there is one issue that is pivotal to the application of emerged and emerging technology to the conventional deterrent it is that of technology transfer. This issue is much more important than is realized, and it is one that is certainly amenable to solution. In the case of the United States, the problem really stems from the multilayered administration of any technology transfer application. Munitions cases are handled by the State Department while non-munitions cases (but ones that have a high degree of technical substance to them such as non-military microelectronics) are handled by the Department of Commerce, with the Defense Department playing an advisory role in both processes. The bureaucracy is cumbersome and should be streamlined, and it is certainly possible to do so.

The role of the Department of Defense is limited by statute to the identification of those technologies that have a security implication. In actuality, however, practice requires that in reviewing such applications, DOD makes solid and fair judgments as to the true military significance of the technologies involved. At present, the people in charge of this process in the Defense Department are not technologists; they are political scientists. They do not know the substance of technology, they do not know the nature of technical developments, and they do not appreciate the fragility of advanced technology and how rapidly it becomes obsolescent unless it is properly utilized.

This has been a major stumbling block to meaningful arms cooperation within the Alliance in the last five years. It has been used by critics on both sides. Some Europeans have politically exploited the issue of technology transfer and its problems. In fact, they have blown the issue completely out of proportion in certain instances. An example is the furor that was raised in some parliaments over the "Specialty Metals Clause" imposed by the U.S. Congress in 1981–1982. The importance of this restriction was greatly overstated in some quarters, and DOD worked hard and successfully to have the clause repealed. Not one purchase from Europe was canceled because of this clause, but the hue and cry was sometimes deafening. The lesson to be learned is that technology transfer should not be considered an emotional issue; it should be handled in a very straightforward manner.

High-level review could easily point out the advantages, both in security and economic terms, and the disadvantages of such transfer. The issue could then be settled in a manner that is consistent with the roles and missions that have been given the various governments by their parliaments. This is not the case at the present time, and, as a consequence, we are not doing the job we should. It certainly will have to be done before we can talk meaningfully about emerging and emerged technologies as major contributions to conventional deterrence in Europe.

It is significant that this important issue of technology transfer involves a "two-way street." Europe has much excellent technology that ought to be applied to U.S. needs, and the United States should make every effort to import it. It is silly for the Alliance to be duplicating the hard-to-come-by research and development resources. President Ronald Reagan's Strategic Defense Initiative, imprecisely referred to in the press as "Star Wars," could very well be the watershed for resolving the issue of technology transfer.

New Conventional Technologies and the Strategic Defense Initiative

Let us consider for a moment the relationship between new technologies for improving conventional defense and the President's Strategic Defense Initiative. Debate has raged since President Reagan made his speech in March of 1983. Most of it has been carried on by people who (1) do not understand the program; (2) do not understand the technology required; and (3) have not thought through the possible consequences. When examined in reasonable detail, and as objectively as possible, it is clear that the initial efforts in the implementation of SDI will be related to surveillance, tracking and pointing. These technologies are ones that have a direct application to a conventional force structure.

The SDI surveillance program objective will permit discrimination between multiple targets, increase the ability to be able to handle the battle management information, and provide a pointing and tracking capability for both incoming and outgoing objects. All of these involve technology with applications to conventional defense. In fact, when the phases of the program being planned at this time are examined, it is obvious that early applications could very well be against conventionally armed tactical ballistic missiles. The kinetic energy missile systems that SDI is undertaking include non-nuclear options and could be in a range of affordability that is comparable to other missile defensive systems such as Patriot, Roland, and Rapier. Consequently, the Europeans should make every effort to participate in SDI in general and should particularly insist on participating in this early phase. In certain instances they should be willing to invest both with their technical talent and their monetary resources. This is not a destabilizing effort—if anything, it is a stabilizing one since it will make the tactical defenses more effective and should make them much more survivable.

Other aspects of SDI are also directly applicable to conventional warfare. Real-time surveillance and targeting information that can be processed quickly and in an unambiguous way with a high degree of reliability is going to provide a distinct advantage to those that have such capability. These are the tasks that are being carried out in the area of battle management by the SDI Organization. It would be prudent for the Europeans to desire to participate in this phase of the research, also.

From a technology transfer standpoint, SDI offers a great opportunity. It is a U.S. presidential initiative, wholeheartedly supported by the Secretary of Defense, one in which the Alliance has been requested and urged to participate. It allows some of the members to allocate resources so they can pursue the unique and particularly applicable phases of the research that are suitable to their technical capabilities as well as to their military needs.

Once a decision is made to participate, the commitment should be contingent on a firm agreement to the terms of reasonable security and technology transfer procedures. That will be the quickest way to get this issue focused and resolved. Without it, there will be a considerable amount of foot-dragging, obscuration, and downright obstruction. The question of access to U.S. companies and technology exchange should be on a company-to-company basis, with the government-to-government role being limited to that of agreeing to the bilateral security agreements, verifying security levels, properly clearing people, and insisting that industrial security be taken seriously by everyone (including the United States). In this way, the situation will be improved for other areas of cooperation—areas not closely coupled to SDI but necessary if the emerging technologies are to be exploited in a meaningful way.

Other Specific Suggestions

We must continue to recognize the fact that there are also emerged technologies. These are technologies, primarily in the electronic warfare area, that are extremely useful and could be exploited immediately, particularly for the rapid upgrading of the NATO forces to enable them to carry out the FOFA mission. The emerging technologies, however—the ones that cover such things as very, very high speed computation, radiation-hardened microelectronics, large-scale integrations in the submicron feature size—all are things that have not yet reached the state of maturity that will let us realistically expect them to make a difference until the end of the decade or a little beyond. They can be instrumental in achieving the Alliance's longer term objective of achieving a capability for the Airland Battle doctrine planned for the next century.

But the emerged technologies, particularly in such areas as anti-jam communications and electronic countermeasures, could be exploited immediately and could indeed make a difference in such missions as FOFA. In addition, these emerged technologies are at a level of technology that makes them suitable for exploitation by the smaller NATO nations. They do not require large capital investments such as those necessary, for instance, for the development of a new weapons platform. They can be applied with small capital investments, and in many cases, they tend to be somewhat labor intensive and therefore could provide much-needed opportunities for additional employment.

Another development that could enhance first-echelon defense was examined in the summer of 1984 by the Defense Science Board of the Department of Defense. It conducted a study that attempted to look at the advantages, disadvantages, values, liabilities, and specific features of urban warfare.[3] This study examined the experience gained from the conflicts that were carried out during the last ten years in the Middle East. Many valuable lessons were learned regarding the ability of troops to defend themselves if urban areas are properly internetted. The study found that there is a distinct difference between trying to penetrate an urban area and trying to defend it. Urban areas have a high degree of inherent survivability, but this inherent capability can be enhanced if troops are properly trained in such

---

[3] *Final Report of the Defense Science Board Summer Study on Urban Warfare*, Washington D.C.: Office of the Under Secretary of Defense for Research & Engineering, January 1985.

tactics and provided with weapons tailored for use in an urban environment.

The Defense Science Board found the demographic development of Western Germany had resulted in a pattern of urban areas that, if internetted, could provide a survivability capability heretofore not assessed. By installing survivable communications ahead of time and by planning for the rapid mobilization of troops specially trained in such warfare, these urban areas can be defended with a degree of survivability against superior first-echelon forces that would considerably enhance the overall level of NATO's conventional deterrence.

If the military would take these concepts seriously and change the doctrine under which they intend to operate in case of a Soviet invasion, many of the problems that exist at present with respect to mobilization could be ameliorated. It appears that with certain minor modifications, the Swedish concept and experience can be applied to the urban/hamlet model. The Swedish reserve structure is configured in such a way that, when mobilized, the forces are assigned to the defense of the areas in which they live. Under this concept, training is less expensive and the mobilization is accomplished more rapidly. As a consequence, urban defense should be more effective.

NATO military planners should be directed to undertake a serious and comprehensive assessment of whether such a doctrine of urban warfare should be a substantive part of the conventional deterrent strategy in Western Europe. It would necessitate taking another look at many of our infantry combat weapon systems, and would probably result in the identification of some needed changes. On the other hand, the problem that this would cause the Soviets would be extreme. Their doctrine of rapid employment of first-echelon forces in a multipronged attack, with equally rapid support by second and follow-on echelons, could quite possibly be blunted to a great degree by such defensive tactics. This issue should be openly debated extensively in order to illuminate its potential.

The Political Thicket

Let us shift now to the area that probably is the most troublesome if one really wants to succeed in raising the level of conventional deterrence. It could be described as facing and getting through the political thicket. The first political question to be answered is whether or not enhancing conventional defense through emerging technologies would provide a greater or lesser degree of stability. To me, it seems obvious that anything that raises the nuclear threshold must be a positive contribution to the underlying political will of any nation, particularly if that improved conventional capability is affordable.

It is paradoxical that worldwide attention is always centered on nuclear forces even though it is evident that nuclear deterrence has worked. One might assume that, should a concerted effort be made to improve conventional forces to the point where they constitute a major deterrent to war in Europe, the upgrading would also be subject to a tremendous amount of propaganda and political debate. However, if the resources required stayed within limits contemplated at present by the Alliance for its security, the chances of a political victory by the Soviets would be much smaller.

The probability of being able to change *existing* defense planning in order to exploit these technologies is very low. Most of the nations of the Alliance operate on a five-year defense plan. Experience has shown that once a five-year plan has been accepted, the ability to make modifications in it is extremely difficult. If emerging technologies had been better understood some years ago, when they were first discussed with governments in the Alliance, a lot of lost time could have been avoided. Instead of trying to have them modify their established plans, the NATO member-governments should have been urged to include accommodation of these new technologies in a sixth year of their five-year plan. If they had allocated resources toward emerging technologies in that fashion, we would be realizing the fruits of such an approach and would now be in the second year of the new five-year plan. Some form of redirection of the planning has to take place.

It must be recognized that from the European standpoint, although security is important, it is not first among national priorities. Jobs often seem to take precedence over security. Consequently, the case has to be made that not only would investment in these emerging technologies improve the security aspects of the Alliance, but it would also produce meaningful employment in areas that could make a difference in the future.

The availability of resources is a problem throughout the Alliance. There are gradations of economic capability as well as of willingness to carry out some of these programs. The Europeans have to rationalize among themselves just how they would carry out some of these technical programs. It is not a simple task.

The present debate on a new European fighter aircraft is an example of the type of problem that has to be overcome. The participating nations have done reasonably well in some commercial projects such as the Concorde and the Airbus, but they have not done as well on many of the smaller tactical weapon systems. There is still too much duplication among the Europeans themselves, and this duplication does nothing but consume resources and delay implementation into the armed forces. The European market collectively is significant, but individual European nations cannot always support the necessary development that must precede production. Here also, the participating nations must learn how to collaborate and must interchange technologies among themselves. Therein lies a bit of the problem regarding successful completion of any initiative.

The Cost of Enhanced Conventional Deterrence

The cost of incorporating the capabilities offered by the emerged and emerging technologies into the NATO conventional military forces in order to enhance conventional deterrence will be substantial, but it appears to be affordable. Since the ET Initiative is a general concept rather than a specific program or set of programs, it is difficult to assign a definitive cost to the entire concept. However, a number of candidate programs, projects, development efforts, and test programs have been identified that could result in the insertion of some of the new technology now under consideration into existing and some newly developed weapon systems—all with the overall objective of enhancing NATO's conventional deterrent posture.

Since, as stated previously, some of these technologies are now emerg*ed* while others are still emerg*ing*, their introduction into the operational forces must be spread over a period of several years. Thus, the cost of the overall effort will not all come this year, or in the next couple of years. There is a general agreement, however, that the technology-insertion programs now being considered can all be realized over the next decade. Some capabilities can be fielded within the next few years, while other less developed technologies may not be available to the NATO operational commands until perhaps the mid-1990s.

Various examinations in recent years of the costs of incorporating the emerging technologies into the NATO deterrent capability have produced estimates in the range of anywhere from $10 billion to $30 billion. Recent DOD studies have suggested that the cost of equipping the U.S. NATO forces in Central Europe with advanced conventional warfare equipment employing the emerging technology in sensors, battle management, and weapons would be on the order of $21 billion. This was based on achieving full operational capability of advanced technology sensor systems for target acquisition, such as JSTARS and PLSS, at a total acquisition cost of around $6 billion; on acquiring better command, control, and communication systems such as JTIDS for NATO battle management and on introducing very high speed computers (utilizing VHSIC technology), and sophisticated battle management systems such as the BETA (Battlefield Exploitation and Target Acquisition) system, which correlates and fuses information from various sensors as an element of the JTFP, all at an estimated cost of about $2.3 billion; and on improving weapons, weapons delivery systems, and smart munitions for anti-armor, enemy rear-area interdiction, and airfield attack, which involve the longest development and test programs and would cost an estimated $13 billion over the next ten years or so. Taken together, these initiatives add up to something over $21 billion over the next decade. A nongovernmental analysis recently estimated the cost of incorporating the emerging technologies into the conventional deterrent capabilities of the Alliance as totalling $22.5 billion.[4]

---

[4]*Strengthening Conventional Deterrence in Europe: A Program for the 1980s*, European Security Study Report of the Special Panel (ESECS II), Boulder, Colorado: Westview Press, 1985.

In terms of the current annual costs of maintaining the NATO forces, an expenditure over the next ten years on the order of $20 billion to achieve the introduction of these emerging technologies as a means of improving and enhancing the NATO conventional deterrent does not appear to be an excessive amount. An average expenditure of a little more than $2 billion per year over the next decade would certainly seem to be affordable if it offers, as it does, a realistic opportunity to raise the nuclear threshold and to enhance significantly the deterrent posture of the Alliance.

Conclusions

NATO must maintain its capability to respond to any Soviet threat "in a manner that neither undermines the firmness of its own governments and peoples nor provokes a resort to force by others."[5] By strengthening the NATO conventional forces thorough the introduction of emerging technologies, the Alliance would realize an increased confidence in its ability to defend against a Soviet conventional attack without the imminent necessity of escalation to nuclear weapons. It would also provide the NATO military forces with conventional warfare capabilities that would signal to the Soviets the probable failure of a conventional attack on the West, thus discouraging any such aggressive adventure.

Contrary to some assertions, the adoption of the benefits of the emerging technologies would not alter the fundamentally defensive posture and strategy of the NATO forces, since none of the improved weapons systems being considered would support offensive operations, and none possess the range to reach Soviet territory. Even in the event of increased tension or crisis, the improvement of the NATO conventional deterrent should have a stabilizing effect on the situation, since a stronger conventional capability would give further assurance that the Alliance would not be forced to escalate to the use of nuclear

---

[5]*Ibid.*, p. 119.

weapons so quickly in the event of hostilities. This would tend to alleviate the likelihood of a preemptive Soviet nuclear attack.

Notwithstanding all the difficulties, the opportunity to improve the conventional force structure and raise the nuclear threshold by means of technology-based improvements is certainly worth the effort. The total cost would be about $20 billion over the next decade. This should become the highest priority of the Alliance for the next decade. NATO should not expend any resources that will not, in a marked way, contribute to the improvement of its conventional forces.

The priorities for selecting the particular programs should be ones that will improve the survivability of our present forces while requiring only a modest change in doctrine, roles and missions. They should be to: (1) counter Warsaw Pact first-echelon forces; (2) to improve counter-air in order to blunt the Warsaw Pact air offensive; and (3) to interdict as early as possible the follow-on forces of the Warsaw Pact.

These priorities are essentially the same as those suggested by the Committee on Defense Questions and Armaments of the Western European Union, as presented in the conclusions of a recent draft report.[6]

This will require a comprehensive program that employs, wherever possible, a high degree of Stealth technology, that uses a highly accurate standoff capability with sufficient range so that the Air Force can interdict deep fixed targets, that has survivable command and control of weapons with increased kill probability systems for the Army's first echelon counterforces, and that seriously considers the utilization and exploitation of the strengths of urban defense to blunt the Soviet's concept of surprise and rapid penetration.

These objectives are generally consistent with the FOFA concept that the NATO command has adopted. The emerged technologies, in particular, can be utilized effectively to realize the FOFA capability rapidly. Achievement of the long-term doc-

---

[6]*Emerging Technology and Military Strategy,* Draft Report, 2nd Revision, Committee on Defense Questions and Armaments of the Western European Union, 30th Session of the Assembly, Paris, May 9, 1985.

trine of Airland Battle will be enhanced if some of the emerging technologies, such as those involving supercomputer techniques, artificial intelligence, etc., are pursued and exploited by the Alliance in a timely manner.

Certain issues must still be resolved if we are going to have any reasonable chance of carrying out such a program. No longer can we configure the threat to match the budgetary considerations. Commitments for a slight increase in resources must be made and the ability to reallocate priorities among those resources provided.

Agreement by the members of the Alliance to participate with the United States in a significant way in the SDI program, would pave the way for solid progress on the question of technology transfer and should be one of the very first and highest priority items. Pressure must be placed continually on the United States to share its technology, and the Europeans must in turn rationalize their development efforts among themselves.

We have in our grasp a very, very important technical capability. It is an advantage we should not squander. Anything that can reduce the real or apparent numerical superiority of the Warsaw Pact must be carried out with dispatch. No less an authority than the rehabilitated Marshal Nikolai A. Ogarkov, former Chief-of-Staff of the Soviet armed forces, has stated that the emerging technologies are going to revolutionize land warfare. He urged the Soviet Army to take it seriously. Let us take Marshal Ogarkov at his word, but let us beat him to the punch. It can be done.

François L. Heisbourg

Conventional Defense: Europe's Constraints and Opportunities

The debate on the conventional defense of Europe is as old as the Alliance and often leaves an impression of "deja vu." There is something similar, for example, between NATO's 1952 Lisbon plan for major troop increases and former West German Chancellor Helmut Schmidt's 1984 proposal to maintain 30 divisions in France and West Germany. However, it would be a mistake to dismiss the present debate on NATO's "Follow-on Forces Attack" (FOFA) strategy and the adoption of "emerging technologies" as simply being the latest twist in Alliance discussions on this subject.

A set of new constraints—budgetary, demographic and political—are affecting the role of conventional forces in the future defense of Western Europe. There are also some novel technological developments that some (mostly Americans) argue could greatly change conventional defense and offense. But Europeans are wary of using technical fixes as answers to political problems—an approach they consider part-and-parcel of American culture. This natural, and probably healthy, European skepticism should not, however, lead to a minimization of the potential effect of technical developments, including those occurring on the other side of the Iron Curtain.

These technological evolutions are taking place in the framework of a geostrategic situation that has been frozen for close to 40 years. During that period, the U.S.S.R. has attempted to "sovietize" the nations of Eastern Europe. Despite, or because of these efforts, the peoples of the "fraternal socialist countries" continue to reject Soviet society and culture nearly two generations after Yalta. Such a conspicuous lack of success for the

Soviet Union after 40 years is tantamount to saying that the U.S.S.R. will not achieve a solid relationship with the East European countries, other than through direct or indirect military means.

In the European experience, the decline of a great empire has always been a dangerous prospect. The U.S.S.R. has in the past attempted to use the existence of its military strength in Europe to further its political aims, as was the case with the SS–20 missiles, and it may do so again. The sense that there is an "impasse" in Eastern Europe may prompt the Soviet Union to enhance its military means of intimidation in order to neutralize deleterious Western influences at work in Eastern Europe.

It is against this backdrop of a failed "post-Yalta" period that one needs to examine the stabilizing, or destabilizing, consequences of technological change, taking into account present and future constraints that weight on the response that Western Europe can make to the Soviet military challenge.

I. Constraints on Western Europe's Defense: Budgetary, Demographic and Political

In the absence of a clear adverse shift in the public's opinion of the Soviet threat and the likelihood of a military confrontation, there is no way in which European *defense budgets* will increase markedly, especially in a context of persistent unemployment and economic recession. This apparently has also become true in the United States.

Europe's record in military expenditures over most of the past 15 years has been comparable to that of the United States, although the trend in the United States between 1980 and 1985 was one of significantly higher increases (Table I). In 1986, real increases in France, West Germany and Great Britain will hover between zero and plus two percent. The figures for the United States in 1986 will be even less encouraging.

The introduction of new conventional weapons will therefore be a long-term process; hard choices will need to be made in de-

TABLE I
Real Increase of Military Expenditure
(percentage)

	1970–1982	1982–1985
United States	8	18.9
France	40	0.0
United Kingdom	28	7.2
West Germany	29	3.3

Sources: (1970–1982) *The Military Balance 1984–1985,* London: International Institute for Strategic Studies, 1984, pp. 156–57; (1982–1985) *NATO's Sixteen Nations,* December 1985–January 1986, p. 87.

fining priorities. This should preclude any spending that does not clearly appear to the European taxpayer to be a direct contribution to the defense of Western Europe. Such could well be the case of certain expenditures related to the Strategic Defense Initiative (SDI).

In the next 10 to 20 years, current and recent *demographic trends* will have an impact on the size and nature of the military forces that can be fielded in Europe. Although largely unnoticed outside the circle of experts, the effects of demographic trends will make themselves felt primarily in the Federal Republic of Germany. The "baby crash," or demographic decline, which began in the Federal Republic in the mid-1960s, produced the 20-year-old generation that currently forms the reservoir for military service. This trend has not only continued, but worsened—the "replacement ratio" has fallen below 1.5 children per family, versus the 2.1 children needed to ensure the long-term renewal of generations—and no upturn is in sight. In terms of both duration and magnitude, the demographic situation in the Federal Republic is the worst in the Alliance and is beginning to have potentially serious military consequences that will make themselves felt well into the first decade of the next century. As Table II shows, the shortfall in available manpower will begin around 1988–1989 and a second sharp fall will occur around l991–1992.

TABLE II

Demographic Situation in the Federal Republic of Germany 1985–1994

Age Class[1]	Total Number of each cohort[2]	Potential draftees[3]
1985	488,000	299,000
1986	473,000	290,000
1987	453,000	278,000
1988	417,000	256,000
1989	365,000	223,000
1990	344,000	211,000
1991	301,000	184,000
1992	265,000	162,000
1993	256,000	157,000
1994	249,000	153,000

[1]Year in which German male citizens become 19 years old (the 1985 age class was born in 1966).
[2]Includes all young men of a given age group whatever their physical, mental or professional aptitude.
[3]Applying present qualifications for military service.

Source: Pascal Boniface and François L. Heisbourg, *La Puce, les Hommes et la Bombe,* Paris: Hachette, 1986, p. 80.

This will result in a nearly 50 percent reduction in manpower within ten years. The West German military and paramilitary forces need the equivalent of an annual intake of approximately 250,000 men to maintain current force levels. If West Germany were to continue to apply present recruitment and selection criteria, this minimum threshold of 250,000 men would be crossed by 1989. Difficulties may occur as early as 1986 because of the shortage of adequately qualified potential draftees. An extension of universal conscription from 15 to 18 months in 1989 and an increase of reserve call-up training are two of the formulas that the West Germans have planned for dealing with this problem. These are rather stringent measures for a post-industrial society in peacetime, it would seem.

The impact on conventional defense will be particularly strong if West Germany is compelled to rely more on its reserves and less on standing forces. This would mean a shift away from the forward-defense, NATO-earmarked *Feldheer*, to the more decentralized, purely national territorial forces (*Territorial Heer*), which have a peacetime strength of only 38,000 men but which can mobilize 300,000 men in time of crisis.

As a consequence it would be logical for the West Germans and the Alliance as a whole to look for possible savings in needed manpower through the adoption of new conventional technologies. On the other hand, these advanced technologies will present problems as they require higher qualifications on the part of recruits to utilize them. For the Federal Republic of Germany a difficult and paradoxical situation will emerge at the beginning of the 1990s:

- There will have to be extended terms of service for young men (both as conscripts and as reservists) and fewer opportunities to apply for conscientious objector status.
- Manpower savings will be sought through the introduction of new weapons systems such as Patriot, which is replacing Nike-Hercules.
- Increased costs will be incurred because of the need to recruit as volunteers and retain as professionals, soldiers to operate and maintain an advanced technology force structure—especially electronics specialists who are already a scarce resource in the West European nations.

These first two measures may be sufficient for handling the manpower shortfall at the beginning of the 1990s. Further on down the road, however, very hard decisions may have to be faced. Troop reductions (not something that the Americans would like) and/or an increase in reliance on the essentially on-call *Territorial Heer*, which could mean a partial retreat from the NATO strategy of forward defense, are possible alternatives that might have to be adopted.

In the other European countries of the Alliance, the demographic situation is not nearly as serious (Table III). The British have a relatively small volunteer force and the French demographic trends remains comparatively healthy. More worrisome

TABLE III

Military Manpower in Europe Standing Ground Forces in West Germany*—1985

	Number	Percentage of Total Number
Federal Republic of Germany	336,000	49.8
United States	205,000	30.3
United Kingdom	55,000	8.4
France	48,000	7.1
Belgium	21,000	3.0
Netherlands	5,000	0.7
Canada	5,000	0.7
TOTAL	675,000	100.0

*Berlin garrisons excluded.

Source: *The Military Balance 1985–1986,* London: International Institute for Strategic Studies, 1985.

from a European perspective is the possibility of a reduction of American troops available for duty in Western Europe. The 18-year-old age-group in the United States will decline from 3.8 million to 3.2 million between 1985 and 1995, with the reduction being strongest among white males (-25%). The all-volunteer force will have to compete for scarcer human resources; this is achievable but will cost money. This would not be particularly alarming were it not for political pressure in the United States for U.S. force reductions in Europe.

The changes in the qualification-needs created by the widespread introduction of electronics into the armed forces, an evolution that is arguably the most advanced in the United States, is an important factor. In the U.S. armed forces the percentage of military personnel trained in electronics rose from 6 percent in 1945 to 22 percent in 1984. What emerging technologies may save in absolute manpower numbers, they may well take back in the form of reduced interchangeability between manpower categories. In the U.S. Army, communications specialists may well outnumber the Infantry by 1990.

These developments in the field of human resources inject a new element into the debate on conventional weapons defense that cannot be underestimated, at least not in the case of the Federal Republic of Germany. Such trends will be a major determinant in the manner in which the West German, and consequently, the French military and political establishments will approach the question of conventional defense. This may also be said to some extent of the Americans, if only because the U.S. forces in Europe operate under both an existing manpower ceiling and the recurring threat of force reduction.

The probability of American force reductions occurring, however, remains low. After all, not only European, but U.S. interests as well, are being served by the presence of forces on the European continent. This is well understood by the average American if one is to believe the current public opinion polls. The rejection of the draft by the American people and the traditional potential for a sudden shift of public opinion in the United States does not, however, allow the Europeans to sleep easily as far as this issue is concerned.

Last, but not least, manpower constraints will also make themselves felt in the defense industries of Great Britain, France and West Germany. There is already a shortage of highly trained engineers and technicians that will impose some bottlenecks on future research.

Analysis has to proceed carefully in any examination of the *political constraints* on European defense, because what is considered as an absolute necessity today can well become tomorrow's taboo and vice versa. Nevertheless, the following can be considered as givens in Europe:

- the persistent attachment of the West Germans to forward defense (notwithstanding increasing demographic shortfalls) and their even more persistent refusal to consider any move toward acquiring a national nuclear capacity;
- the continuing French posture of being in the Alliance and outside of the integrated command of NATO, despite the progressively stronger degree of empathy with the Federal Republic;

- the continuation of nuclear force modernization in Great Britain and France, as well as the continued stationing of British and French conventional forces in West Germany at their present levels.

On the other hand, a certain number of political conditions are in a state of evolution in Europe. For example, the Franco-German rapprochement is indicative of what may well be a sea change in French political and doctrinal attitudes toward the defense of West Germany. In the past France considered the Federal Republic as a buffer zone rather than a "blood brother." This new Franco-German "alliance within the Alliance," raises new questions, not so much in terms of potential European-wide defense policies than in terms of the problems of establishing an acceptable modus vivendi between a bilateral Paris-Bonn defense relationship and NATO's integrated structure. West Germany, after all, is the only country that has earmarked all its standing divisions of the *Feldheer*) to the Supreme Allied Commander Europe (SACEUR).

The renewed acceptance of nuclear deterrence as a necessary evil of European security is another recent change. During the year preceding the deployment of Pershing IIs and cruise missiles in Western Europe, the balance of terror was not a popular topic, even outside of pacifist circles. Only France escaped, by-and-large, this general trend. The resolution of the debate on intermediate-range nuclear forces (INF) through the introduction of the "Euromissiles," despite the massive efforts of the so-called Peace Movement, calmed things down. Deterrence is once again respectable. The Strategic Defense Initiative also helped to focus many minds back on the fundamental contribution of nuclear weapons to peace in Europe. This has been true most of all in West Germany, but it can be said of all Europe.

There is a growing sense in Western Europe that the U.S.S.R. has definitely failed in its historical mission of sovietizing its Eastern European sphere of influence. Nobody in Europe would draw the conclusion that there is any prospect that these countries will be able to exercise their right of self-determination freely in the foreseeable future. But the Soviets still face a troublesome future in Eastern Europe as opportunities for Western ideas and influence grow in that region. The resulting climate will not be one of Western vulnerability. However, the politico-economic decline of an empire combined with its continuing military strength does not make for a very stable situation.

Finally, there is an increasing realization that Western Europe is in grave danger of dropping out of the world competition in high technology, particularly in those areas relating to electronics and data processing. This is compounded by the understanding that losing out carries heavy economic, social and political penalties as manifested in the loss of productivity, unemployment and dependency. Here again, SDI has certainly helped to make people concentrate on the problem. Attitudes toward new conventional weapons will also be shaped by this "Eurorealism," which signifies that Europe must regain its position in hi-tech research and production.

II. Emerging Technologies: Evolution or Revolution?

The question of whether so-called emerging technologies[1] represent evolutionary or revolutionary change is somewhat clouded by the confusion that is sometimes created between the technical aspects of this question on the one hand and the overall impact on the theater-wide military balance on the other. In my opinion, the answers are quite different for each category.

There are cycles in technological evolution just as there are in many other fields of human enterprise; technical progress is not linear. To take a relatively recent set of examples, the 1930s and 1940s witnessed a revolution in technological change; the invention of radar, the jet engine, ballistic missiles, are some major landmarks, not to mention the splitting of the atom. From the

---

[1] "So-called" because many of these technologies have already emerged (i.e., there is already widespread use of microelectronic components, digital signals and data processing).

1950s to the 1970s, constant improvements were made on the basis of such innovations. The potential for further incremental improvement in those is limited, so in many cases these inventions now show reduced yields per unit of money spent.

This has translated broadly into an exponential increase in the unit cost of major weapons systems, and conversely, a reduction of the absolute number of systems fielded in the framework of a given budget. Combat aircraft are a prime example of this trend (Table IV). Some experts have facetiously predicted that at the present rate of unit cost evolution, the U.S. Air Force could afford to buy only one new aircraft per year by the middle of the next century. But, there is no example of this sort of process continuing unabated to such an absurd end: new weapons systems and/or technical breakthroughs based on different physical principles always alter the situation, either through the elimination of preexisting systems (i.e., horse cavalry at the turn of the last century) or through their radical change.

Today a revolutionary period is in full swing. The building blocks of this new period of radical change are to be found in the electronics field:

- electronic mainframe computers (mid-1940s);
- transistors (late 1940s);
- integrated circuits (late 1950s);
- microprocessors (early 1970s).

The combination of these elements has made further breakthroughs such as minicomputers, massive number-crunching capabilities, and low-cost memories possible. Further down the road, one can foresee high performance, moderate-priced expert systems and symbolic processors, complex software generation, etc.

These breakthroughs will have two consequences for conventional weapons development. First, they will radically increase the effectiveness of *individual weapons systems*. "Smart" weapons or precision-guided munitions (PGMs), based on new technologies, started to appear on the battlefield in a significant

TABLE IV
Total Combat Aircraft*

	1970	1985
U.S. Air Force	6,500	3,700
French Armée de l'Air	500	475
R.A.F.	720	599
Luftwaffe	980	586

*Strategic nuclear forces excluded.

Source: *The Military Balance*, 1970–1971 and 1985–1986 editions, London: International Institute for Strategic Studies, 1970 and 1985.

fashion at the end of the Vietnam War (e.g., the destruction of the Doumer Bridge on the Red River with laser-guided bombs) and they nearly swung the course of a major conflict for the first time during the Yom Kippur War in 1973.

Such weapons have now been perfected: the Falkland Islands conflict demonstrated the cost-effectiveness of standoff missiles (Exocet AM–39), and anti-aircraft rockets (Rapier, Roland). The next generation of weapons, such as the European third-generation anti-tank missile (Trigat) or supersonic anti-shipping missiles (the Franco-German anti-naval supersonic, ANS, successor to the Exocet) will incorporate major innovations, such as a true "fire-and-forget" capability. During the 1990s, introduction of self-homing individual munitions or submunitions on airborne short- or long-range standoff missiles (SRSOM, LRSOM) or ground-based multiple rocket launchers (the European-American MLRS phase III)[2] will greatly enhance the threat to the opponent's ground-based assets. The combination of aircraft

---

[2]Terminally-guided anti-armor warhead developed by U.S. (Martin Marietta), French (Thomson-Brandt), West German (Diehl) and British (Thorn-EMI) firms.

with accurate standoff missiles of different sorts may represent one of the means through which air power may escape from its present rather infernal unit-cost spiral. It is clear that an adversary equipped with evermore effective and "user-friendly" weapons will have an advantage over one who is not so equipped, all other factors being equal—this last caveat being essential.

Second, technological breakthroughs provide the potential for a vast increase in the effectiveness of conventional forces that could result from the "real-time" communication, command, control, and intelligence-gathering (C^3I) of weapons systems interconnected as *combat systems* at battlefield or even theater-wide levels.

Even more so than with smart weapons, it is here that the potential gap between the haves and have-nots can be spectacular. In the 1973 war, the Israelis, after the severe punishment inflicted initially on their tank and air forces by the PGM-equipped Egyptians, were able to vanquish their adversaries, inter alia, through the exploitation of the lack of coordination between Egyptian units. More significantly, the Israelis destroyed, with hardly any losses, a major proportion of Syria's Air Force and surface-to-air missiles through a highly integrated, close-to-real-time, C^3I system during the Israeli invasion of Lebanon in 1982.

A talk with those military corps commanders of the French Army[3] who are equipped with a state-of-the-art mobile battlefield communication system (RITA or Réseau Intégré de Transmissions Automatiques) gives a sense of the greatly enhanced flexibility provided by integrated and real-time communications. In a contest between two roughly equal forces with similar levels of training, experience and luck, the commander of an army equipped with such a system has a decided edge over his adversary: hence modern C^3 can be a powerful force multiplier. The British, with the Ptarmigan communication system, are similarly equipping their Army on the Rhine. The U.S. Army

---

[3] At present, the two corps of the French First Army stationed in West Germany and Eastern France.

is planning to do so in the framework of its Mobile Subscriber Equipment program. This is not to mention other ventures in various areas of C^3I, such as:

- JTIDS (Joint Tactical Information Distribution System)—interconnects NATO ground and air communications networks, which includes links to and from the 18 NATO Airborne Warning and Control Systems (AWACS);
- PLRS (Position Location Reporting System)—has an accuracy of 15 to 25 meters;
- JSTARS (Joint Surveillance and Target Attack Radar System)—is to be airborne and used for the surveillance of ground-based assets;
- JTFP (Joint Tactical Fusion Program)—fuses U.S. army intelligence into the framework of the "deep strike" concept.

It is tempting to ascribe a revolutionary effect to C^3I that enables the more effective use of existing fire and manpower resources, especially if these assets are managed in conjunction with smart weapons. The combination of time-efficient C^3I with cost-efficient smart weapons may well change the nature of a conflict in a high-threat environment to the point where a small number of precise weapons and munitions and a correspondingly lighter, logistical "tail" would be used along with short, swift manuevers, resulting in a potentially rapid decision.

One must not be overly optimistic as many of the programs in the C^3I field are on the drawing board rather than in the field. The software entailed by an efficient C^2 (not to mention C^3I) system is horrendously complex to generate if one wants to be sure the system works in the field without crippling "bugs" popping up. It took the French and the Belgians close to 15 years to develop and field RITA, and the time-frame for the development of Ptarmigan was similar for the British. During the 1970s, the U.S. armed services failed in their attempt to set up Tri-Tac (Tactical Communication Program) as a system embracing the battlefield and theater C^2 of the three services, hence the need for the U.S. Army to look at systems derived from RITA and Ptarmigan. An excess of technical ambition runs high risks in this area.

84 / The Conventional Defense of Europe

Another drawback is that C^2 and C^3I systems are themselves vulnerable to enemy countermeasures, offensive electronic warfare not being a weak point of the Soviet war machine. The "fog of war" will probably continue to reign in real-world battle situations.

In addition, the usefulness of such systems will remain limited if interoperability with other Alliance communication networks is not factored in during upstream development. This is not always the case; downstream or ex post introduction of interoperability does not yield optimal results.

Despite these observations, the gradual introduction of microelectronics at the weapons level and macroelectronics at the battlefield or theater level will produce gradual but deep changes within both force structures and employment concepts. This is very much the case with the French Force d'Action Rapide (FAR) and is demonstrated by the new French interest in mobile massed anti-tank helicopter warfare. Evidence of this change can also be found in at least parts of the U.S. Army (e.g., the light Infantry division concept and the so-called "technological" division).

There is an element of paradox here: the Europeans, essentially the French and the British, have taken major steps toward adopting the new, more mobile conventional defense resulting from the combination of smart weapons and mobile battlefield C^2. They have not, for their own reasons, made much of the politico-strategic question of these shifts, treating them rather as natural adaptations to the new state of the art. The Americans, on the other hand, have strongly pushed concepts such as "Airland Battle"[4] even though the U.S. ground forces remain by and large probably more cumbersome, excessively reliant on firepower, and less adapted to maneuver warfare than some of their European counterparts. This American propensity for elaborating concepts first, then selling the relevant weapons systems second, has some resemblance to the "missionary/trader" sequence in nineteenth-century Africa.

---

[4]Airland Battle is the official U.S. operational doctrine, as contained in the Army's *Field Manual 100–5*. It stresses maneuver warfare and deep thrusts.

Before examining the possible consequences of conventional weapons defense on European-American and intra-European relations, it may be useful to evaluate the potential effects of emerging technologies on the military balance in Europe.

III. Balance of Forces: No Quick Fixes

The momentum and the reach of the Soviet defense effort offer little hope to those who might expect emerging technologies to help restore the military balance without an improbable upward shift of gears in the Alliance's own defense spending. By calling for real increases of four percent per year as a way to redress the balance through the introduction of new conventional weapons, SACEUR has given a clear indication of the limits of the benefits of emerging technologies. Even if one takes into account the dubious reliablity of some of the Soviet Union's East European allies, the balance is unfavorable to the Atlantic Alliance, as is demonstrated in Table V.

This table gives very much a "best case" for NATO since it presupposes that countries such as Denmark or the Netherlands, whose military prowess has been somewhat limited in the past couple of centuries, would be staunch allies, whereas East Germany or Czechoslovakia would refuse to take arms. It does not deal with the qualitative balance, where NATO has some significant advantages. On the other hand, Soviet budgetary levels are now such that, even at low rates of increase, the quantitative turnout of Warsaw Pact matériel remains vastly superior to that of the West. During 1984 the Warsaw Pact produced 1,070 tactical combat aircraft compared to NATO's 525, and 3,650 tanks compared to 1,760 for NATO. Such a two-to-one situation is not reassuring.

The diverging evaluations in the West concerning the balance of power have less to do with such figures, at least as orders of magnitude, than with the relevance of counting hardware as a means of evaluating a correlation of forces. Critics of this approach point out that a balance does not exist for itself, but as a

TABLE V
NATO vs. U.S.S.R. Force Balance in Central and Northern Europe

	NATO[1]	U.S.S.R.[2]
Divisions deployed	20⅓	37⅓
(Tank divisions)	(12⅓)	(14)
Main battle tanks	8,799	24,200
Artillery, MRL	4,235	14,800
Anti-tank guided weapon (launchers)	1,292	2,660 *est.*
Surface-to-air missiles (launchers)	527	2,800 *est.*
Ground attack fighters	1,194	1,915

[1] Area covered includes West Germany (excluding French forces stationed there), Belgium, Luxembourg, The Netherlands, Denmark and Norway. Includes all allied forces stationed within the area.

[2] Area covered includes East Germany, Poland, Czechoslovakia, and the four westernmost military districts of the U.S.S.R.

Source: *The Military Balance, 1985–1986,* London: International Institute for Strategic Studies, 1985, pp. 186–87.

function of strategic objectives: those of the Alliance being purely defensive. Hence the corresponding allied force counts and postures are not strictly comparable to the Warsaw Pact's order of battle. However, this does not allow one to assume, a priori, that the conventional force balance is in a state of equilibrium.

It may be useful here to recall some of those arguments that tend to minimize the imbalance, and to comment on them. Such a review bears out, in my opinion, the continued need to strongly rely on nuclear deterrence to back up the intrinsic weaknesses of conventional defense in Europe:

A successful breakthrough would require the aggressor to have at least a three-to-one force superiority, which does not clearly exist today in Europe. This is true in the area where the breakthrough is to take place: force concentrations may even have to be much higher than a three-to-one ratio. However, this is not so at the theater level. In May 1940, France and Great Britain faced a similar number of German divisions on the Western Front but were defeated by a swift blow dealt in a limited zone of action (The Ardennes and Sedan). Reliance on a purely conventional equilibrium is not something Europeans should look for. Only through the existence of nuclear deterrence, which discourages military adventures of the pre-1945 variety, and through the prevention of local force concentrations, can we live with any degree of equanimity with an imbalance in conventional forces. However, the nuclear peace can be kept only if the potential aggressor fears the use of nuclear weapons in the event of war: this precludes no-first-use postures.

Smart weapons will allow one to block an aggression; the number of the aggressor's tanks should not be compared to the number of the defender's tanks but should be related to the number of the defender's anti-tank weapons. The West will come out ahead in new hi-tech defensive weapons. First, it should be noted that the Warsaw Pact has a strong superiority in the number of anti-tank weapons. Second, and this fact is not without links to the preceding observation, battles are won by the combined use of arms, not by a single category. During the Yom Kippur War, the Israelis lost a first battle due to the surprise effect of Egyptian PGMs versus tanks and aircraft. The Israelis adapted to the circumstances and used U.S. PGMs that had been rapidly airlifted to Tsahal, winning the war by the combined use of armor, PGMs, superior tactics and C^2. The Soviets adapt similarly: the deployment and PGM-equipped attack helicopters in Europe and the massive use of infantry combat vehicles illustrate this trend in terms of matériel. The new Soviet emphasis on "operational maneuver groups," which exploit points of enemy weakness in a target-of-opportunity mode, is a translation of this in the tactical offensive area. Troop concentrations and axes of effort will be less predetermined than in the past, thanks to the new possibilities opened up by helicopter transport and other developments.

Last, the Soviets are not losing in the race toward modern armaments. For example, they deployed a first generation of smart weapons (SAM–7, Sagger ATGW, etc.) at approximately the same time as the West. This is not an encouraging precedent, although the gap may be more difficult for the U.S.S.R. to bridge when it comes to software-intensive C^3I systems.

Through more stringent controls of technology transfers to the Warsaw Pact countries, the Western countries may well create difficulties for the Soviet military R&D effort. It would nevertheless be imprudent in view of past and present experience to expect the Soviets to lag significantly in deploying weapons systems. It would hardly be less reckless to expect such a lag to endure, since as far as C^3I is concerned, at the very least, the Soviets have good expertise in electronic countermeasures.

A defense in depth, based on "islands of resistance" equipped with PGMs, will prevent an adversary from capitalizing on his initial gains. This would have the added advantage of being a "non-provocative, defensive defense." This view is often expressed by German analysts, if only because of historical experience: from 1943 to 1945, the Wehrmacht fought a long series of defensive battles in the U.S.S.R. against tremendous odds, using such islands of resistance. An updated version of this defense, would call for a galaxy of urban "hedgehogs" hitting away at the adversary with pre-stocked fire-and-forget anti-tank and anti-aircraft weapons; enemy tanks would be largely neutralized in an urban environment.

However, one cannot transform overnight a peace-, comfort-, and nature-loving population of reservists into a mass of battle-hardened combatants, inured to the most extreme conditions of chemical and conventional warfare. Such a territorial concept also presupposes that West Germany would definitely expect to lose a portion of its territory since "defensive defense" implies the absence of counterattack capabilities. Strangely enough, this concept seems to be more "à la mode" in West Germany than in France. Strange because France's size and geographical position would make this strategy somewhat less absurd for it than for West Germany, where a third of the population lives less than 70 miles from the Iron Curtain.

The U.S.S.R. could not initiate an attack without bringing its forces to a war footing through visible preparations. The interval would be sufficient to mobilize the West's superior overall resources. This has been true and probably still is to a large extent. An attack out-of-the-blue would not allow the Soviets to throw a sufficient portion of their conventional forces at the allies; they could not be confident of a lightning victory, even with the benefit of surprise, unless of course they used tactical nuclear weapons on a large scale. This remains a highly unlikely prospect because of its suicidal potential. Nuclear deterrence thus remains of the essence here.

Present trends, however, are not all reassuring for the Alliance for a number of reasons. In terms of quality, Soviet-deployed weaponry is often comparable to, if not better than, that of the Western nations: tanks, artillery, and increasingly, infantry combat vehicles and helicopters. The technical superiority of the allies' combat aircraft is narrowing. A comparison of human resources does not allow one to reach definitive conclusions. Much is made of the dreary life of Soviet soldiers, as portrayed in the pseudonymous Victor Suvorov books,[5] and their demoralization in Afghanistan. However, one should be wary of drawing military conclusions from such descriptions. Some of the 500,000 U.S. troops in Vietnam were demoralized, drug-addicted, fragging-prone and were not much more impressive than the 100,000 soldiers occupying Afghanistan. One can also mention the grave problems of morale that pervaded the U.S. forces in Europe at the height of the Vietnam war. Rough-hewn *kholkozniki* may not be worse soldiers than some of the low-IQ, underskilled recruits of the difficult opening years of the American all-volunteer force. Comparisons in this area are most difficult to make, if only because morale is largely a function of action and success. Weaknesses of Soviet pilots and sailors are known, as is the relative lack of independent leadership capabilities at the junior officer level; the West may hope to benefit, especially if Soviet plans go wrong. However, only the test of battle could allow us to weigh these factors, especially since much can be said of countervailing deficiencies on the Western side (e.g., our pilots are better than theirs, but we have so few of them, etc.).

In the area of weapons systems and tactics, the Soviets could attack with smart armaments in lieu of tactical nuclear strikes. Such conventional attacks would have, as a corollary, the ab-

---

[5]See, for example, *Inside the Soviet Army*, New York: MacMillan, 1982.

sence of significant warning time. This possibility has at least a positive political offshoot in that to some extent it erases the distinction between "first" (e.g., West Germany) and "second" line (e.g., France) states, thus in theory favoring a joint response to a common threat. As far as airland combat is concerned, the Soviet stress on operational maneuver groups reduces the escalation option of flexible response: a defender will very much hesitate to cross the nuclear threshold against an enemy already ensconced in the heart of the defender's territory, and probably intermingled with its forces and populations.

Furthermore, the possession of accurate conventional weapons used in a coordinated, real-time fashion may open a wholly new option to an aggressor in the opening stages of a conflict. At present, the Soviet Union could probably not launch a purely conventional attack that would: (1) decapitate a major and predictable proportion of NATO staging points, depots, lines of communications, C^3 centers, airbases and ports; (2) avoid prospects of high attrition to its forces; and (3) reduce civilian casualties to a minimum, so as to limit the risk of massive retaliation by NATO.

Therefore, the early recourse to nuclear and chemical weapons remains an option inherent in the Soviet force structure, maybe even increasingly so (e.g., the large-scale introduction of nuclear field artillery since the end of the 1970s) because conventional forces are not able to achieve any of the above missions.

With improvements in terminal guidance and target acquisition, the instruments for a preemptive strike by standoff air-to-surface missiles and short- to medium-range conventional (ballistic or cruise) surface-to-surface missiles could exist within the next 10 to 15 years. Such a Soviet version of Offensive Counter-Air would be especially ominous since it would be quick, decapitating, and could introduce doubts about the credibility of significant reprisals by the Western countries: it could be the Soviet way of slipping under the nuclear threshold.

Such a Soviet surprise attack capability would not only be of military significance but would also be a major political component of the global correlation of forces. Western Europe would be subjected to a regime of permanent intimidation, with the achievement in the conventional field of what the SS–20s did more modestly in the nuclear area. In the latter case corrective measures were technically and financially quite accessible, if not politically easy to implement.

The threat of conventional surprise attack remains hypothetical as long as the corresponding technology is not fielded. But it cannot be discounted, given the accuracy and the performance with which the exponents of deep strike and Offensive Counter-Air credit their own potential capabilities. A strike against predetermined targets in the European theater would be particularly enticing if it were conducted as a surprise attack, unclouded by the fog of war and unmarred by NATO preparations and countermeasures. This poses a potentially serious doctrinal problem, both for the NATO-integrated countries and for France. For those countries that have endorsed the doctrine of flexible response, a new area of Soviet escalation dominance may well appear for which there is no easy solution. A NATO tactical nuclear response to a Warsaw Pact surgical conventional attack may well be disproportionate; conventional preemption by NATO of a Soviet offensive would be politically unacceptable. Countermeasures, such as anti-tactical missile defenses, could be a way out, but at a cost. France's nuclear doctrine would also find itself at pains to bridge the gap between a militarily limited, low-collateral-damage Soviet attack and recourse to the threat of mutual nuclear annihilation. A country that relies on a "weak to the strong" deterrent posture cannot afford to appear non-credible in its nuclear posture. This point was made by the former French Chief-of-Staff, General Jannou Lacaze, in his valedictory speech at the Institut pour les Hautes Etudes de la Défense Nationale in May 1985:

> The attack of our fixed installations—Albion, strategic bases, pre-strategic missile depots, command posts, communications centers—by ballistic or cruise missiles with conventional warheads represents a new threat which we must take into account, all the more since an aggressor could be led to believe that their use would not be considered a major attack and would not give rise to massive reprisals.[6]

---

[6] See *Défense nationale,* July 1985, p.22.

This sort of "decapitation" through conventional means would represent a new and grave evolution of the Soviet threat. Such a surprise attack option will call for a significant upgrading of Western Europe's air defense.

At this stage, the only certainty is that the side lacking smart weapons and integrated combat systems, and the appropriate doctrine for their use, will be worse off than before. Little hope, in a piecemeal and gradual conventional modernization process, can be pinned on arms control to make up for Soviet progress. The Mutual and Balanced Force Reduction talks have since 1972 served to prevent U.S. and West German troop reductions as well as block significant Soviet troop increases—not an unimportant achievement, but not one that allows us to expect conventional arms control to succeed in anything other than holding actions.

Confidence-building measures may be diplomatically and politically appealing, as well as militarily useful for our countries, and should therefore be vigorously pursued at the Stockholm conference. Provisions that could make a surprise attack less feasible and increase warning time cannot hurt. However, previous experience has taught us that militarily significant confidence-building measures remain improbable; the growing capability of the Soviet Union to initiate an aggression after only a short and ambiguous warning period will have to be faced by effective military countermeasures.

Selective employment of chemical weapons by an aggressor would also complicate the allies' options. Modern chemical weapons can be used in a precise and highly efficient mode—against air bases, for example. NATO, or France, may have a credible declaratory policy that relies on nuclear weapons to retaliate against a large-scale, population-destructive, chemical attack, but such a retaliation would be much more difficult if chemical strikes were limited to narrow targets with little or no collateral damage. An air base or a tank unit can defend themselves against chemical weapons but only by incurring a very sharp degradation of their combat capability. Since U.S. stocks of chemical weapons in West Germany will apparently cease to be useful within a few years, the adversary might consider that he will be able to launch chemical attacks without risking similar retaliation and, consequently, without even having to adopt highly penalizing chemical defense measures. This is a difficult, gruesome subject, which the Europeans need to address without waiting for the Americans to force them to do so, especially in light of the recent U.S. decision to produce so-called binary chemical munitions. After all, this is a problem affecting, first and foremost, European territory. Because of these different factors there will probably be a gradual reduction of warning time, and this problem will be complicated by the more-often-than-not ambiguous nature of such a warning. In history there are examples of surprise achieved not through secrecy, but rather by the defender's disbelief, misinterpretation or wishful thinking.

Finally, geographic location is an added negative factor. The 218,000 U.S. Army personnel based in Europe represent some 28 percent of total American Army effectives. In all, the 323,000 U.S. troops present in the European theater comprise 15 percent of all U.S. military personnel. If the forces earmarked for intervention in Europe are added to these figures, they still fall short of the Soviet deployments. Geography is basically responsible for this situation, and there is little prospect of modifying current U.S. force dispositions. That consideration does not, however, make things easier for the West Europeans located on the rim of the Eurasian landmass. At most, only a few hundred miles separate the Iron Curtain from the Atlantic Ocean. It must be remembered that close to two-thirds of the Soviet Union's ground and air forces are turned toward the European theater, a significantly higher proportion than U.S. assets deployed in the same area; and Soviet back-up forces are a train- or truck-ride away from the theater. In contrast, continental U.S. forces have to cross several thousand miles of hostile air and sea space to get to the European theater.

For all these reasons, Western Europe will remain, in the foreseeable future, dependent upon U.S. ground forces and the American nuclear guarantee to make up for the fundamental imbalance in favor of the Soviet Union.

IV. The United States and Europe: The Unhappy Alliance?

The introduction of new conventional weapons and systems poses two principal sets of problems for European-American relations: (1) agreement, or disagreement, on doctrine and strategy; and (2) cooperation, or lack of cooperation, on the new military tools and the technology on which they are based.

Doctrine and Strategy

As is so often the case in matters relating to the common defense within the Alliance, there is a tendency on the American side to develop new concepts well in advance of the large-scale deployment of the systems on which they are supposed to be based. Although in principle it would be inappropriate to criticize an approach in which "thought precedes action," the fact remains that, in practice it usually is unsafe to build vast doctrinal edifices as long as the relevant technology has not been, to some extent at least, proved in the field. What some Americans may have seen as a "watering-down" of Airland Battle and deep strike by timid Europeans, was in part an expression of realism; Follow-on Forces Attack, as a result of the pressure of the integrated allies, is probably closer to reality than some of the more theoretical and radical long-term U.S. concepts.

To this disparity between U.S. and European doctrinal approaches must be added the frequent suspicion on the European side that new concepts are sometimes a question of intellectual or political fashion, and that such fashions have a habit of coming and going rather quickly. They also happen to serve commercial interests. These observations should in no way serve as a justification for the manifestations of some particularly European shortcomings such as a lack, in some of the more "integrated" countries of NATO, of self-reliance in elaborating concepts on their own. The answer that NATO doctrine is a collective product of multilateral consultation is too often a nice way of qualifying incremental or, ex post facto, European input vis-à-vis U.S.-inspired plans. FOFA would probably not have existed in the absence of American-originated concepts. In other cases, the lack of European-initiated input can be traced to precisely the opposite reason, e.g., French refusal in the past to elaborate European-wide military concepts. This has fortunately begun to change, both at the theoretical level with the Franco-German defense dialogue established in 1982, and in practical ways with the setting up of the French Force d'Action Rapide and associated measures.

An assertive American overflow of concepts and a European timidity or aloofness, are themselves a poor basis for a healthy relationship. When one looks at doctrinal differences per se, the situation is neither novel nor better.

As usual, the basic disagreement is about the relative roles of nuclear deterrence and conventional defense. For the Europeans, the repudiation of conflict remains central: any war in Europe would be a holocaust. The quickest way to have an unacceptable nuclear exchange would be to start out with a conventional conflict. This should logically preclude any move toward a policy of no-first-use of nuclear weapons that posits a return to the pre-nuclear age of "acceptable" military conflict.

On the American side, there is the understandable wish not to be in a position where extended deterrence could place the national territory at nuclear risk. This unresolved and unresolvable debate has been the bread-and-butter of Alliance politics and misunderstanding for most of its lifetime. Emerging technologies and "conventional deterrence" only give a new twist to this contradiction: for a Frenchman, this is a "rien de nouveau a l'Ouest" situation, although it is perpetually rediscovered.

The debate has, however, now taken a new course. On the one hand, it has been somewhat defused by SACEUR's handling of the conventional forces issue. Initially, during the 1982–1983 period conventional force improvements were often being portrayed as a possible substitute for nuclear weapons. Subsequently, a lower profile was adopted: FOFA does not have, at face value, the political and military flaws in a direct transposition to Europe that Airland Battle and Counter-Air 90 do.

Follow-on Forces Attack is a conventional maneuver "sub-concept" of flexible response, whereas Airland Battle calls for the integrated use of conventional and nuclear forces and the conduct of offensive operations on the enemy's territory. The question of the congruence between FOFA (for NATO in Europe) and Airland Battle, (adopted by U.S. forces) has been conveniently sidestepped despite (or because of) the fact that NATO's supreme commander in Europe and the U.S. commander for Europe are one and the same person.

On the other hand, the debate on the proper role of nuclear versus conventional forces has been complicated by the extraneous concept of SDI. All other comments on "Star Wars" aside, the Strategic Defense Initiative has anchored, rightly or wrongly, the idea in parts of Europe's political and defense establishment that there is a fundamental shift occurring in American thinking with regard to extended deterrence.

SDI could mean the long-term dismantlement of nuclear deterrence from the "top-down," the new conventional concepts causing the erosion of deterrence from the "bottom up." This attitude is relatively prevalent in France[7] and is certainly not restricted to traditionally left-wing and/or anti-U.S. segments of the body politic.

The question of conventional defense retains, however, a good deal of latent virulence, which could flare up in unforeseen ways. The transition of SDI from pure research to actual development could set off a larger quarrel on the conditions of deterrence within the Alliance—a remake on a larger scale of the Franco-American disagreement on SDI at the May 1985 Bonn summit, for example? The debate would be particularly divisive if it were conducted in the context of possible unilateral U.S. and/or West German force reductions.

Trans-Atlantic difficulties do not usually have the dire consequences that have been inevitably predicted ever since the dispute over the European Defense Community (EDC) in 1952–1954. Unhappiness seems to be a fact of life of Alliance relations that does not produce quite as unhappy results. For example, the failure of the EDC anchored Great Britain's troops in West Germany; the rejection of former President Charles de Gaulle's "directoire" proposal in 1958 led to the establishment of an independent French nuclear force; the debate on the deployment of the American INFs left the Soviets faced with Pershing IIs and cruise missiles, etc. In the same way, the almost simultaneous appearance on the scene of new conventional defense concepts and SDI has done a great deal to remind many Europeans of the

---

[7] See, for example, Pierre Lellouche, *L'Avenir de la guerre,* Paris: Éditions Magazine, 1985.

real merits of nuclear deterrence after the pacifist paroxysm of the early 1980s.

Trans-Atlantic Cooperation

The growing perception of the limits of America's nuclear security guarantee and the consequent rediscovery of Europe's vulnerability has apparently put the West Germans and the French on converging paths. Such a convergence between Paris and Bonn may be encouraged by the way in which European-American cooperation on emerging technologies is handled. European complaints about the lack of a true "two-way street" are well known. Apart from the special case of France, there is a traditional imbalance between the United States and its European partners in mutual arms procurement. During 1984 France achieved a slight surplus in its military trade balance with the United States,[8] but according to one American source, between 1979 and 1983 U.S. military exports to NATO Europe totaled $11.4 billion, while only $1.4 billion at most was sent in the opposite direction.[9]

The reasons for this trade imbalance, which need not be examined in detail here, are worth mentioning:

- the difficulties of competitive bidding in the United States with the tremendously cumbersome and uncertain American procurement process—the failure of the transfer of the Franco-German Roland anti-aircraft system to the U.S. Army in the 1970s is a perfect example of this;
- the existence in Europe of major areas of dependence on outside sources of military hardware—this is especially true in the smaller countries, but also in some of the medium-sized states such as Italy and Germany;

---

[8]The total volume of U.S.-French trade in the armaments field is much smaller than either U.S.-West German or U.S.-British transfers.

[9]*World Military Expenditures and Arms Trade 1985,* Washington, D.C.: U.S. Arms Control and Disarmament Agency, 1985, pp. 132, 134.

- the long-term choices to which certain European countries have committed themselves—the F–16 fighter and Trident II D–5 submarine-launched missile system are two of the costlier items involved.

New conventional weapons, and more especially the cutting-edge elements regrouped under emerging technologies, will exacerbate these long-standing difficulties. This is due, first of all, to the sheer scale of the research and development effort that must go into these systems and the share of R&D in the total cost of a system increases with time. About 30 percent of the cost of the fighter aircraft of the 1990s will be for front-end R&D expenditure, more or less double that of the predecessor aircraft conceived in the 1960s.

Second, such trends will force drastic choices upon Europe's defense industry in terms of mergers, partnerships and other joint ventures. The temptation will be strong for our American partners to attempt to split the Europeans rather than to favor intra-European rapprochements, which are, in many cases, a necessary step toward a balanced trans-Atlantic relationship. The United States, with its vast, unified, internal arms market and its giant defense industrial corporations, is especially well placed to compete with European countries and firms that only in exceptional cases are of world-class size and world-market performance, the French being once again generally better off than their neighbors. To use an allegedly Japanese catchphrase "In business, small is not beautiful; small is just small."

Third, there is the enormous scale of the American defense R&D effort, which has increased by some 50 percent in real terms since the end of the 1970s, and which today represents about two-fifths of overall U.S. R&D spending, both public and private. These expenditures are of a completely different order of magnitude from those of the Europeans. American public and private military related R&D expenditures today are approximately $45 billion per year, compared to $3 billion for France and $1 billion for West Germany.

The increase and scale of U.S. spending will obviously produce results, not only in areas related to SDI (the overall impact on military R&D of which remained marginal until fiscal year

1986), but in technologies fundamental to future conventional defense. Moreover, it would be a mistake to belittle the scope of the five-year SDI research program. The $26 billion that is to be spent between 1985 and 1989 represents more than ten years of total French or British military R&D expenditure (including development spending).

There is little time left for the Europeans to put their act together, both in terms of organization and of funding, if they wish to be true partners in developing the combat systems of the 1990s—this is especially true for West Germany. Even though the Federal Republic's military R&D funding has increased by close to 30 percent in 1985, it will take several years for Bonn to catch up with the French or the British in this realm.

The challenge may well be compounded by recent developments in U.S. technology transfer policies, which could have damaging industrial and military, not to mention political side effects. In the wake of American and European excesses of the 1970s, the United States has been pleading with vigor and some success for a badly needed tightening of technology transfers toward the Soviet bloc. There is obviously much to be said for hampering Soviet efforts to develop and field state-of-the-art conventional weapons.

France has pursued a similar policy. The discovery by French intelligence at the beginning of the 1980s of the cost-efficiency evaluations drawn up by the Soviet military industrial commission (VPK)[10] on technology transfers from the West came as a major shock. The stiffening of national release procedures, the revival of the Coordinating Committee for Multilateral Export Control, and the creation of a group of military experts by the COCOM countries are the growth of a justified heightened concern.

---

[10] The VPK is the inter-ministerial Soviet body in charge of, inter alia, planning and assessing technology transfers from the West. Civilian (international trade affairs), military, scientific (State Committee for Science and Technology, the Academy of Sciences) and intelligence (KGB and GRU) agencies work in conjunction with the VPK. See Henri Regnard, "L'URSS et le Renseignement scientifique, technique at technologique" in *Défense nationale*, December 1983, pp. 107–121; and, "Soviet Acquisition of Militarily Significant Western Technology," U.S. Department of Defense, September 1985.

Distressingly, it is at the very time when serious progress is being achieved by the United States and its partners in COCOM that restrictions have been imposed on intra-Alliance technology transfers. Previously unclassified briefings have been closed to allied personnel who have already been cleared by their own authorities. Programs of Alliance-wide defense interest such as VHSIC (very high speed integrated circuits) have remained barred to allied countries and firms for inordinately long periods of time. The British, for obvious reasons, have been more unhappy than most about it and have been the most vocal about their unhappiness.

The free flow of data, controlled by reciprocal security agreements in the case of sensitive areas of technology between allies, is in NATO's best interest: the strength of the West lies very much in the synergisitic effects obtained through a high degree of transparence. Certain reactions in Great Britain, and to some extent in West Germany, leave one with the impression that if the United States were to impose major restrictions on its allies, this issue could be one of the principal stumbling blocks in European-American cooperation on new conventional defense. Such restrictions would induce enhanced intra-European cooperation rather than the growth of trans-Atlantic ventures.

The strong push by former British Defense Minister Michael Heseltine in favor of European defense industry cooperation is certainly a sign of the change in attitudes. The French, less accustomed to relying on others, have not been particularly surprised by U.S. trends. This climate facilitates, in theory at least, converging views on European collaboration in the area of new technologies.

V. Europe and Emerging Technologies: Now or Never

For the sake of clarity, the intra-European consequences of innovation in conventional defense will be reviewed under the categories of: concepts, military organization, and armaments policy. In practice, however, the three categories are rarely dealt with separately at the political level, notwithstanding the existence of distinct forums such as the Independent European Program Group (for arms and technological cooperation) and the Western European Union (in the political field).

Toward European Initiated Concepts

Despite the existence since 1963 of the Elysée Treaty between France and West Germany, defining common strategic concepts, the beginning of a continuing Franco-German politico-military dialogue started only in October 1982. Until then, initial West German reticence (under pressure, whether actual or feared, from the United States) and French shyness or aloofness had effectively prevented the establishment of a bilateral body composed of both civilian and high-level military officials entrusted with defense and security issues.[11]

A Franco-German commission on security and defense was set up at the end of 1982, but the extent to which it has touched on basic strategic issues should not be overestimated at this stage. The difference of status vis-à-vis NATO integration and the fear of upsetting, in the case of France, a much appreciated defense consensus has made progress inevitably slow. What is most important at this stage is that the Franco-German process has removed taboo subjects: for example, the notion of prompt forward defense by French troops in West Germany or the expression of a "common security" concept between Paris and Bonn are now hardly the subject of debate. The anathemas that abounded some years ago have ceased to exist. The circumstances that in 1976 forced then-French President Valéry Giscard d'Estaing to backtrack from expressions such as the "espace militaire Européen unique" (the single European military area) are unlikely to reappear.

Barring delays caused by internal political developments, such as an increasing degree of paralysis within the West Ger-

---

[11] For a description of the Franco-German dialogue on defense and security, see "Les Relations Franco-Allemandes et le fait nucléaire" by André Adrets (pseudonym) in *Politique Etrangère,* no. 3, (Autumn), 1984 and the ensuing discussions in the following two issues of that publication.

man government or a lasting uncertainty about France's political future after the spring 1986 French parliamentary elections, the ground seems to be laid for relatively broad initiatives in terms of strategic concepts. These could most easily be taken in the field of new conventional defense, if only because it has been, up until now, devoid of the deep passions that exist in the nuclear arena.

If new concepts for conventional deterrence are to be adopted, several conditions must be fulfilled simultaneously:

- The French public must accept a major shift in French strategic thinking from defense based upon "l'Hexagone" (a term designating the metropolitan territory, since the country is roughly shaped like a six-sided geometrical figure) to a European-wide defense; recent public opinion polls as well as most political reactions to the Force d'Action Rapide and the "alliance within the Alliance" concept point in that direction. Only the Communist Party (ten percent of the vote) remains hostile to the Franco-German rapprochement.

- Politicians and the public in West Germany must understand that France will not return to the fold of an integrated NATO. No event in the past 20 years has given cause to any French government to change its country's separate status: there would be a lot to lose and little to gain for France if it were to do so. The balance sheet would not be much better for the Alliance if France became a pacifist-riven, politically weakened, new integrated partner. This is probably better understood in Bonn since the 1983 Euromissile crisis, when France remained a bulwark of pro-nuclear, pro-Alliance and pro-defense sentiment.

- The United States must adopt a benign attitude. The Franco-German rapprochement on defense concepts may be unpleasant (and a West European-wide common position even more so) for people who are used to dealing with their allies in piecemeal fashion, but it is in the long-term American interest to have a more self-reliant Europe as a partner. Washington has the power to prevent Europe from coalescing, if only through the de facto influence it wields on West Germany by ensuring that country's security. Bonn can make no positive move toward common European positions on defense if the United States has strong objections. Incidents, such as the intervention of the State Department's former head of European affairs requesting that the Western European Union (WEU) political directors not discuss certain security issues raise concern.[12] The same is true of the understandable, but shortsighted attitude of individuals in segments of the U.S. defense industry who fear the disappearance of arms markets in Europe.

- Last, but not least, there must be an understanding between the Franco-German team on the one hand, and the other Western European countries on the other, concerning the necessity of a synergistic effect between a bilateral process and a multilateral rapprochement. In practice, this means: (a) that Bonn and Paris must never leave the other European countries behind; (b) that the others must not attempt to split the special Franco-German relationship, born of a tragic history and an inseparable geography; and (c) that a lot is to be gained from mutual emulation. The political revitalization of the WEU would not have happened without the Franco-German rapprochement; similarly the reactivation of the Independent European Program Group (IEPG) would not have occurred in the absence of British and Dutch encouragement stimulated by Franco-German cohesion.

Organization of Forces

New conventional weapons will greatly affect force structure. The introduction of mobile, real-time, secure battlefield communications in the Belgian, French, British and eventually American armies, and the deployment of large numbers of helicopters carrying anti-tank missiles on both sides of the Iron Curtain are portents of these changes.

France, through a unique convergence of political constraints and operational lessons, has gone further than most in modifying its military organization to adjust to the imperatives of new conventional defense. This is somewhat paradoxical for a coun-

---

[12]See Bridget Bloom's article "U.S. warns Europe on independent defence stance," in *The Financial Times*, April 2, 1985.

try that has not endorsed NATO doctrine in this area and that remains, more than any other, openly wedded to nuclear deterrence. (This happens more often than not. Between 1978 and 1982 France was the only major European country consistently to attain the NATO objective of a plus three percent real annual increase in defense spending). The Force d'Action Rapide, conceived at the beginning of 1982 and fielded in the summer of 1985, was largely born of the recognition that forward defense could be implemented in a politically acceptable way through the use of highly mobile transport, communication and combat equipment.

At the same time, the evolution of Soviet doctrine has made a rear-based, forward-attacking force desirable in itself. Attacks after an ambiguous alert based on the breakthrough and infiltration of operational maneuver groups in unforecastable directions call for flexibility rather than standing in a quiet part of a hypothetical front line, which the Soviet version of deep strike will make untenable.

The setting up of the FAR with its 200-plus combat and tactical helicopters has been paralleled by a trimming-down of ground forces from 312,000 to 290,000 (compared to West Germany's 336,000 and Great Britain's 160,000) through a reduction of service units in favor of combat troops. The FAR remains, as the rest of the French Army, reliant on conscription. Greater technical competence and combat readiness have, however, tended to reduce the proportion of draftees and to prompt the creation of so-called long-term conscript volunteers in 1983. These are draftees who have decided to stay in the force, with improved pay and conditions, from 6 to 12 months beyond the normal one-year period. Today they represent more than ten percent of the annual intake of conscripts. The reform of the French Army with its increased professionalism runs counter to those theories that propose reliance on the massive use of conscripts and reservists, as in Helmut Schmidt's suggestion for 30 French and West German divisions. With huge forces, money would be lacking for either smart weapons and rapid transport or to implement certain German "non-provocative defense" concepts. Moreover, the latter would give smart weapons to the offspring of a peaceful postwar West Germany to fight in isolated, enemy-surrounded "hedgehogs," as if they were the equivalent of seasoned Third Reich soldiers with three winters of combat experience against Stalin's Russia.

The creation of the FAR has pulled France into a quite specific military dialogue with its partners. This was, of course, already the case with the French First Army and especially its 48,000-man Second Corps based in West Germany both before and after France left the integrated structure of NATO. The Ailleret-Lemnitzer agreements with SACEUR in 1968 and the Valentin-Ferber agreements with the Commander-in-Chief of Allied Forces in Central Europe in 1974 bear witness to this. But the First Army has a geographically limited sphere of action, whereas the FAR, by its very nature, has theater-wide potential.

This means that issues involving conventional forces find themselves right at the heart of Franco-German relations and are to some extent independent of West Germany's integrated status in NATO, especially since logistics remain a national prerogative even in the integrated countries. Matters such as air cover and conduct of operations would logically come under the framework of France-NATO relations just like those that now exist for the French First Army. Given the central position of West Germany in France's defense posture in Europe, there is little doubt that Franco-German consultations will play an essential role in such arrangements.

Two important questions arise with regard to future force organization in the Central European context in view of the evolution of the Soviet conventional threat toward shorter warning times, the existence of defense spending and demographic constraints, and the spread of emerging technologies: (1) What protection should Europe attempt to devise vis-à-vis the modernization of Soviet conventional aviation and rocket forces and (2) is forward defense sustainable beyond the next ten years, given West German demographic trends?

With respect to the question of protection, a whole tier of the existing NATO air defense barrier will be obsolete before the end of the next decade despite the introduction of new defensive systems. Yet the conventional first-strike capability that the Soviets can expect to possess by then will need to be faced. Major doubts remain as to the systems that the U.S.S.R. will favor for this task. Aircraft with long- or short-range standoff missiles? Air- or ground-launched cruise missiles? Terminally guided SS–21s, SS–22s and SS–23s? This is an area in which conceptual work needs to be done quickly. Hard choices will have to be made knowing that it will take more than ten years to develop a new ground-based air defense system with some anti-missile capability and will take considerably longer to devise a dedicated anti-tactical ballistic missile system. In this last case, cost effectiveness is not a foregone conclusion. This whole area of air defense, which is dealt with in the Alliance framework by all 16 member states, has to embrace not only active systems (e.g., SAMs, artillery) but also, and maybe even more so, "passive" measures—hardening of hangars may not be spectacular but it certainly increases the survivability of the Alliance's aircraft. The same may be said of the introduction of a new aircraft identification system (NATO Identification System), which may help us to avoid shooting down our own aircraft.

Regarding the second question on force organization, forward defense may not be easy to sustain. Even if West Germany is able to implement the decisions extending the duration of the draft, prolong call-up reserve training, draft women, and stiffen grounds for exemption from military service, etc., it remains doubtful whether all of these measures will be sufficient to continue the manning of the 12 standing divisions of the *Feldheer*. If that were to become the case, the Federal Republic would be facing truly hard choices: either new ways to preserve forward defense or to experiment with "alternative" formulas.

In this respect, defense in depth based on the attrition of the adversary by a large number of urban or rural islands of resistance that are manned by reservists equipped with smart weapons is not particularly convincing. A Swiss or Swedish defense model not only requires a certain tradition—how many West German "Greens" would be ready to spend three to four weeks under arms each year for a large portion of their adult life—but it also supposes a relatively marginal, second-line, geostrategic situation. If the Swiss or the Swedish armies have not been put to the test since Napoleonic times, it is also because these countries were not prime targets or even means to larger aims. Nazi Germany could live with neutrals which allowed exports (Swedish iron ore etc.) or the transit of strategic goods (the

German-Italian link through the St. Gotthard tunnel). The Federal Republic does not enjoy the option of neutrality. A form of reinforced territorial defense in West Germany would signify less a move toward neutrality than a shift toward depending on Soviet benevolence, unless—and only unless—the wider security of the Federal Republic continued to be guaranteed by the stationed forces of other nations.

It would no doubt be difficult to convince these nations to assume the burden of forward defense if there were a West German retreat from that doctrine. Even if "neutrality" were not intended by a new doctrine of "defensive defense," it could well be interpreted as such by the allies and, more dangerously, by the Soviets; such a concept could be very destabilizing. The talk about such "alternative concepts" should not evoke great enthusiasm in the West German population at large, since "territorial defense" would entail the sacrifice of major portions of West German territory and population, with no hope of recovery.

Last, but not least, it would be wrong for the Americans to minimize West German manpower difficulties by citing the Israeli example. Israel combines a small territory (facilitating quick call-up); a justifiably high perception of a military threat, which has materialized massively several times since 1948; and an extremely "offensive defense."

These observations point to no remedy to the West German situation, short of recommending a "pro-birth" movement in the Federal Republic. The United States, France and other countries should, however, examine with West Germany the military options necessary to maintain forward defense at its present level of credibility, thus avoiding a lowering of the nuclear threshold. Emerging technologies will help, but more, such as U.S. force redeployment and/or new types of French participation beyond the FAR, may be needed.

Given these needed changes in the force structure, what are Europe's chances of developing the corresponding military hardware and combat systems?

European Armaments Industry?

The challenge represented by the rapid expansion of American defense and R&D expenditures in the first half of the 1980s is well understood by most European governments and defense firms. The IEPG, created in 1976, was upgraded to the ministerial level in November 1984 and has decided to extend its scope to upstream technological cooperation. Bilateral memoranda of understanding on armaments cooperation have been agreed upon by all parties. France alone has signed general intergovernmental agreements with seven countries (Greece, Italy, Spain, Denmark, Portugal, Belgium and The Netherlands in less than three years; this is over and above its preexisting links with West Germany and Great Britain). The French and the West Germans have given a major push forward to their traditional armaments cooperation by starting in 1983–1984 on the development of the third-generation anti-tank missile (with the U.K.), the future combat helicopter and the ANS missile, (the supersonic successor to the much publicized Exocet family of weapons). These and other responses, such as military spinoffs from the projects under the recent EUREKA initiative, are necessary steps in the right direction.

Major obstacles remain, however, and must be overcome if the Europeans are not to be reduced to filling only limited niches or becoming mere subcontractors as more and more emerging technologies effectively emerge:

- The nature of postwar industrial reconstruction in Europe has created historical links between the U.S. armed forces and U.S. firms on the one hand, and European armies and firms on the other. More often than not, cooperation between European firms does not come as naturally as trans-Atlantic collaboration. In the electronics field, out of 100 agreements made by European firms, 50 are established with U.S. companies, 30 with Japanese firms and only 20 with other European corporations.[13] The absence of an agreement between the three militarily most important European countries on the "Eurofighter" of the 1990s is a spectacular and unfortunate

---

[13]Press conference by the Chairman of the French Professional Electronics Trade Organization (SPER), February 6, 1985.

example of the difficulties the Europeans have in organizing themselves.
- U.S. firms, with their long domestic production runs and U.S. government-financed R&D, are in a strong position to lure the European armed services, especially in a context of rising up-front R&D costs.
- The Europeans have been unable to establish any sort of common defense market. Competitive bidding frequently may not be open to foreigners in the United States, but it is even less frequently open to foreign European firms in any given European country (at least, when there is an indigenous producer in the running).
- Last, but not least, European military R&D spending needs to be increased, primarily in West Germany but in all other countries as well. This means allocating an increased share of slow-growing defense budgets.

Other measures, such as pre-competitive cooperation (e.g., the technological cooperation program within IEPG) and upstream international military-industrial definition of joint programs, need to be intensified if Europe, and its defense industry, is to avoid duplication of effort and have a serious chance of making its own choices in new conventional defense.

The future of air defense is a significant illustration of this, because of the need to make decisions in the near future. New conventional weapons in the air defense role will largely rotate around:

- A replacement need—that of the American HAWK surface-to-air missile, which after many upgrades will have expended its improvement potential by 1995, 40 years after its inception; the same is true of the aging British Bloodhound system.
- An operational need—that of a medium-range surface-to-air missile (fitting in between the long-range, high-cost, Patriot and short-range systems such as Crotale, Rapier and Roland), which will have to fend off the Soviet's end-of-the-century conventional air threat (a combination of aircraft, air-to-sur-

face standoff missiles, and surface-to-surface short-range missiles).
- A strategic reality—the conventional Soviet threat is largely focused against the European theater, whereas U.S. territory remains largely immune to this type of aggression. There is some logic to a European attempt to cope with this threat through the use of indigenous concepts and hardware, while continuing to cooperate with the United States, whose troops in Europe are directly dependent on air defense.

Hence NATO's air defense should be considered as a priority item by the Western European nations, if its cost-efficiency is demonstrated, since the Soviet acquisition of a conventional deep strike capability against predetermined targets has been made possible by their emerging technologies. This carries with it no doctrinal revolution: such an adaptation to a changing threat has little to do with a Star Wars-like pretense of decimating swarms of nuclear warheads. Conventional air and missile defense is certainly something that the Europeans need militarily, know how to do technically, and can bear politically. This is so provided that the cost-efficiency ratios are similar to those of current air defense, the appropriateness of which is not questioned in any of the European countries.

Apart from a nascent French medium-range surface-to-air program, this issue has been largely avoided, particularly by West Germany. Even though the Luftwaffe's Chief has expressed such a need,[14] and the notion of an anti-tactical missile defense has been aired by West German Minister of Defense Manfred Wörner,[15] force of habit has prevailed until now. If the Americans invented the HAWK and the Patriot in the past, why worry about the future—"They'll come up with a new product."

Such psychological attitudes have provoked effects as dissimilar as France's defense policy of self-reliance, on the one hand (this has probably been a "plus" for all but may in time cease to

---

[14]Interview with General Eimler in *Jane's Defence Weekly*, March 23, 1985.

[15]See Richard Halloran, "Bonn Urges New Missile Defense," *The New York Times*, February 10, 1986.

be economically sustainable in an essentially national framework) and West Germany's destabilizing wave of pacifist youth in search of identity and security, on the other. The latter type of political alienation is not in the Alliance's interest.

The evolution of the conditions of conventional defense in Europe has created major opportunities for a more coherent European posture. The Franco-German rapprochement, the widespread feeling that it is time to put Europe's act together in the field of defense, the reappraisal of France's doctrinal attitudes and force structure—all these are, at least in part, attributable to the challenge of conventional defense requirements.

Europe obviously needs to fulfill these obligations. The divided continent, unreconciled to its division and serving as the depository of the world's largest accumulation of foreign and indigenous weapons and forces, is a natural candidate for oblivion if defense and security matters are mismanaged. Europe also has the technical skill and the economic base today that should make it very much more an equal partner of the United States within the Alliance. The success of European arms exports and the superior performance of European weapons systems in significant categories (short-range air defense, battlefield communications, main battle tanks, etc.) point in this direction. It would be a tragedy for Europe and probably a disaster for the Alliance if this chance were to be wasted. It is the primary responsibility of the Europeans to seize it.

The United States has the power to prevent Europe from grasping this opportunity. Either by exerting pressure and protesting against Europeans working together in purely European forums or by playing on the fears induced through the threat of removing U.S. troops from Europe, the United States could break efforts toward European solidarity. Conversely with American acceptance, the Europeans could make the most of circumstances forced upon all by the pace of technological change.

Andreas von Bülow

Defensive Entanglement: An Alternative Strategy for NATO

Ever since the Soviet Union broke the U.S. monopoly in atomic weapons, Western defense doctrine has suffered from a credibility gap. "Massive retaliation" with its "tripwire" function for conventional ground forces had to be superseded by the strategy of "flexible response." Since then, deterring an attack on Europe has relied on what is termed the triad of deterrence, consisting of conventional armed forces, limited-range nuclear weapons in Europe, and nuclear weapons of intercontinental range. Confronted with this triad, the adversary should be uncertain as to what countermeasures he would have to contend with in an attack. NATO, in its own eyes too weak to sustain a sufficient conventional defense, reserves to itself the first-use of nuclear weapons as a means to offset the Eastern superiority in men and matériel.

The risks in current NATO strategy reduce its credibility. Charles de Gaulle was among the first to question the reliability of extending the American nuclear umbrella beyond the United States to Europe. If the Soviet Union were to attack Copenhagen, Hamburg, Milan or Athens, would the American president respond with nuclear weapons if such an action could lead to the nuclear destruction of large parts of the United States? Would the use of atomic weapons be contemplated at all, given the threat of a nuclear winter in the Northern Hemisphere? Conversely, the Europeans wonder about the consequences of nuclear hostilities for Europe and West Germany in particular. Given the incredible quantities of destructive means amassed by both the West and East in Germany, could not the spark of a war in parts of the Third World leap over to Europe and set off a nuclear war? Could not the decades-old tension and conflict between the two superpowers yet explode in a war limited to Europe?

The peace movement and the American president are searching for ways out of the dilemma in almost identical terms. There is mounting pressure for a change in the strategy of flexible response. The West must set about developing a convincing strategy of avoiding war in the East-West relationship. And it must adapt and develop its military structures and armaments according to this strategy. Linked as it is to nuclear deterrence, the conventional side of such a strategy is of an importance that can scarcely be overestimated. No one wants to make conventional wars in Europe feasible again and hence thinkable. Still, in the event of war, an inadequate conventional defense capability could lead to the use of nuclear weapons. And the threat to use nuclear weapons would not prevent the other side from responding in kind or even raising the ante. This creates mutual terror. Thus it is that offsetting conventional weakness by threatening the use of nuclear weapons is credible only to a very limited extent. New ways must be sought and found to escape from the dilemmas of the present strategy.

New technologies, especially those of microelectronics and sensors, afford new possibilities for developing weapons that hold great promise for conventional defense. The spectrum of items that can be developed in the industrial laboratories ranges from mines to small combat and reconnaissance drones to cruise missiles and advanced missile technology. With these enemy runways, aircraft, bridges, traffic junctions, radar facilities, in fact whole command centers, can now be pinpointed, neutralized and destroyed by conventional means. We will be able to equip the simple infantryman on the battlefield with relatively inexpensive arms that within seconds can shoot down sophisticated equipment or destroy heavy armor worth millions. This technology will also make it possible to render the adversary blind and directionless in a matter of minutes. Never before have science fiction concepts been so close to the prospect of realization.

On the other hand, there is the danger that the simple allure of new military technology will divert our attention from its wider ramifications. Every weapon not only has a tactical application, but is an integral part of a broader military strategy. And this strategy must be rationalized within the overall political perspective, which includes foreign and security policy, détente and disarmament policy, and even trade policy.

As history reveals, often inconspicuous and primitive weapons developments can have extraordinary consequences—consequences rarely contemplated originally. Thus, pikes and crossbows in the hands of mercenary armies spelled the end of the medieval system of knighthood. It took centuries before this was understood in all the countries of Europe. The machine gun of the First World War revolutionized infantry operations, but the military long found it difficult to recognize this. Hundreds of thousands of dead were the consequence of the assault tactics no longer justified when troops were mowed down by the new machine gun. The inevitable answer was the tank. Now guns could be brought into position by troops protected from the hail of bullets. That such a fast, land-mobile weapon made it possible to paralyze the enemy defense with lightning speed was grasped by a minority in the German Wehrmacht. They were able to persuade Hitler to give the tank priority, whereas the French and British commands, to the woe of Charles de Gaulle and Basil Liddell Hart, stayed with the outmoded tactic of incorporating the tank into infantry units. The crushing of French resistance within a few days in 1940 was the consequence. Today, it is becoming manifest that the main weapons system of past offensive operations, the tank, will ultimately get caught in the increasingly sophisticated web of modern anti-tank defense technology.

New technologies in weapons are, then, nothing new. Yet the many new concepts in recent years such as "Airland Battle" in conjunction with the promise of "emerging technologies" and even the departure from the doctrine of mutual assured nuclear destruction in the Strategic Defense Initiative, indicate substantial pressure for change from the established strategy of flexible response. Amid all the ideas and theories now debated we must take care that we are not dragged by purely military or engineering decisions in political directions that either the Western Alliance as a whole or the Europeans do not deem desirable. Europeans in East and West want to prevent conventional wars. But they would also like to be safeguarded against the danger of careless and premature escalation into an atomic exchange. The nuclear threshold should be markedly raised. This is believed to be achievable only through a substantial improvement in conventional means.

I. The Political and Military Balance in Europe

Most of the fierce differences of opinion over the strengths and weaknesses of a particular strategy or the value of individual weapons systems ultimately have their origin in very distinct assessments of the Soviet Union, the Warsaw Pact, and the East-West relationship in general. What course will the Soviet Union plan for the decades ahead? Are the Soviets principally motivated by a grand strategy for world revolution or by more narrow, state interests? How dangerous today still are such plans of world revolution? Can the U.S.S.R. remain a superpower if its own economic development no longer provides the basis for such a role? How free of or dependent upon the Soviet Union are the East European states in domestic and foreign affairs? To what extent can East European leaderships govern without any consideration for the people? In what direction should the East-West relationship develop so as to further the interests of Europeans, East and West? What are the possibilities for change and where do we hit the bedrock that neither the West nor the East can clear away?

First of all, it should be noted that none of the nations of the NATO Alliance, but also none of the Warsaw Pact nations, including the Soviet Union, wants to wage war in and over Europe. Whether one of the alliance systems is capable of directly or indirectly imposing its will on the other by the use of military force will be discussed later. But if those on both sides want to avoid war under any circumstances, why then can they not manage to transcend the Iron Curtain so as to reduce the extreme provocation created by the military machinery of both camps and begin balanced force reductions?

Only one who quite naïvely believes the glossy literature of NATO will attribute the guilt solely to the East. Naturally the changing, though ultimately incompatible, social orders confronting each other remain a constant source of difficulty. Yet every layman knows that the East is at the point of losing strength because its economic basis has fallen off sharply in comparison with the Western nations.

There is no question that the communist system is out to foster world revolution or rather to change the balance of power in its interest, wherever it is afforded an opportunity. But it is debatable whether it has much success in doing so. There is also the question of whether in all its strivings it is prepared to accept risks that even remotely resemble those that, for example, Hitler was prepared to run with his assaults to the west and the east. The answer is no. As a matter of course, East and West alike vigorously exploit the elements of weakness on the other side. Cadres are trained, advisers provided, and matériel openly or covertly supplied for surrogate wars. Direct intervention, however, has been rare. Afghanistan is one example; here, it seems to me the interest in keeping a nation previously friendly to the Soviet Union from straying into the sphere of influence of China or even the United States provides the explanation for the brutal intervention. On the other hand, we must acknowledge that the Soviet Union has by treaty placed the status of West Berlin, with its extremely imperiled access routes, largely beyond dispute. The city's exposed geographic situation has not been changed by this, but legal constraints have been clamped on any inclination to exploit the situation by acts of blackmail. Today one must break treaties to gain one's ends.

We West Europeans must recognize that the West has not been able to exploit to the slightest degree any dissatisfaction, however great, among the people of Eastern Europe. The military suppression of all uprisings within the strategic and political glacis gained by the Soviet Union in 1945, first against the people of East Germany, then Hungary, then Czechoslovakia, and the failure of Western help to materialize indicates clearly that military means cannot be used for intervening across bloc lines. The risk of escalation into a world war involving a nuclear exchange would be the unacceptable consequence.

The evolution of the communist system, not its destabilization, should be the aim of the West. To increase the maneuverability of the East European peoples, we in the West must maintain a fine security balance. For the Soviet Union, Eastern Europe is above all a security glacis (won with 20 million casualties in World War II) over which attacking Western armies would first have to advance in order seriously to threaten the Soviet Union. Since the Russian Revolution of 1917 there have been countless attempts at destabilizing the Soviet state. There was the shameless exploitation by the Germans of Soviet weakness immediately following the revolution. The 1917 peace of Brest-Litovsk, which was terrible for the Soviet Union, sanctioned the ceding of extensive territory from the present-day Soviet Union. At the time numerous Anglo-American landings and military interventions were attempts to deal the new regime its deathblow. A few years later the Hitler invasion brought the Soviet Union to the brink of the abyss. With the immense breadth of the country, the support of a population welded together in resistance, the aid of large American industrial supplies, and not least a huge death toll, the U.S.S.R. was able to defend itself. The generation of politicians who experienced or suffered through all that will have little inclination to abandon voluntarily the glacis they so dearly won. This is quite apart from the fact that the continued existence of communist governments in Eastern Europe has now become a challenge to the prestige of the Soviet Union as the leading power. Any attempt by the West to gain political, and especially military, advantages through destabilization of the communist systems of Eastern Europe will always be stifled anew with military means by the Soviet Union.

The West's strategy and military structure should work toward processes of relaxation in the Eastern bloc. We in the West will make progress only when, in Soviet eyes, the Eastern security system does not appear threatened. It is at this point that we find the link between emerging technologies and concepts such as Airland Battle. Of course, under no circumstances can the West undermine its own security through carelessness or pacifistic impulses; it must remain vigilant. The West must make sufficient sacrifice for its defense. This defense must be highly effective. Adventurist acts are out of the question. Yet it would pay to consider which tactical and strategic military changes from our present situation tend to promote an evolutionary process in Eastern Europe and which tend to prevent it.

My argument is that we should forego procuring weapons that compel the Soviet Union to perpetuate its iron-handed hold over the glacis of East European nations. The West should, and this at least applies to the West German contribution to NATO, transform its armed forces into a structure that is less capable of territory-gaining ground operations than at present. The Soviet Union, as well as some among our Western allies, surely fear one thing: that the Germans, dissatisfied with their political situation since the end of the war, could also become militarily restless if a situation of military weakness were to develop in Eastern Europe. From today's perspective this concern is unfounded. Yet the concern should also become groundless by virtue of the military structures to be adopted in the future. By the nature of their military configuration, the nations of Europe should consciously make themselves incapable of launching an offensive war to seize territory in Europe.

One question will surely be raised, especially from the American side: Can and should we strive at all for a policy of conciliation with the Soviet Union? There are those who regard the Soviet Union as the embodiment of evil on earth and anticipate the final battle of good against evil. However, because there must be a common interest in preventing nuclear catastrophe, there is simply no alternative but to seek conciliation. Whether in the constant ups and downs of East-West relations all events can always be managed to the satisfaction of both sides remains to be seen. But we must get the process of joint management under way.

Worst-case scenarios are misleading. In this endeavor it is of little help to take the worst-case scenarios as outlined in the security debate as the basis for foreign policy considerations and long-term military strategy, since they are misleading. We must strike a balance between those, primarily in the military, who think in security policy terms and keep the worst case in mind and those who favor judicious cooperation with the Soviet

Union and the states of Eastern Europe. This surely includes taking into account the legitimate security interests of the Soviet Union. In return the Soviet Union should be expected to pursue a policy within its sphere of domination that accords the East European nations more political latitude for shaping their own affairs. That this road is not entirely closed is shown by the examples of Hungary and in part Bulgaria, two countries under far less pressure from the Soviets to conform than are the German Democratic Republic (G.D.R.) or Poland, which at present are still of prominent strategic importance for the security of the Soviet Union. But in Poland, too, the Soviets are gnashing their teeth in vain.

Economic, and military, inefficiency in the communist system. But has not the Soviet Union, by arming itself in recent decades far in excess of its own security needs, created a condition that makes disarmament or even arms limitation virtually impossible? Without any doubt, the Soviet military apparatus is impressive, and the West must maintain its defenses. On the other hand, we should not be hypnotized and attribute to the Soviet "bear" qualities that he does not, or simply cannot, possess. In the Western mind there has taken root a schizophrenic way of perceiving Eastern Europe and particularly the Soviet Union. If the Soviet Union or any one of its allies proclaim great advances in the economic or scientific spheres, practically no one in the West is prepared to lend credence. However, should an Eastern announcement of this sort pertain to military capabilities, then such reports are taken at face value in the West. No one appears to ask whether a military apparatus can so completely divorce itself from the inefficiency of the economic and social systems surrounding and supporting it. The inefficiency of the overall system is a bottleneck for the military system too.

No one in the West assumes that every soldier or every unit of the Bundeswehr gives precisely the military performance the regulations call for. This is just as much the case for the U.S. Army and the other allied forces. There are enormous differences between what ought to be and what is. Surely it is no different in the Red Army. The so-called "operational maneuver groups," for instance, may in their ideal conceptual form foster the demise of traditional frontal fighting in favor of commando-type units that penetrate deep into the enemy hinterland and collapse the defense from behind. In reality, however, the Soviet army, consisting of 75 percent conscripts and hence extremely thin on leadership, is no more capable of performing this feat than the whole of the U.S. forces or the Bundeswehr. A society that promotes private initiative so little and stakes nearly everything on centralized planning cannot realize the opposite ideal in the military sphere. All our intelligence and observations confirm this.

Quite similar considerations apply to supplies and equipment. A tank engine does not differ essentially from a truck engine. A country like the Federal Republic that is a leader in the technology of motor construction also builds good tank engines; the durability, low maintenance, and economy are evidenced in both types, the military and the civilian. Conversely, a country that tends to struggle with problems in manufacturing motors will scarcely achieve the state of the art in the construction of tank engines either. Thus the Soviet Union has yet to build engines equal to those of the West. Soviet "borrowing" of technology from among the West Europeans and Americans speaks for itself. But their unsolved problems with metallurgy alone impede the Soviets from latching on to the West's standard of performance.

Superior Western economic capabilities. We must considerably temper the Western claim that the performance of Warsaw Pact military technology is roughly comparable to that of the West since the performance of Soviet matériel, especially in the wars in the Middle East, tend to belie this view. We should also simply bear in mind the relative overall economic strengths. In population figures alone, the West European nations comprising NATO surpass the Soviet and East European nations. Together with the United States and Canada, the Western Alliance has nearly double the population. In a protracted conventional conflict, say in the form of a traditional war of attrition, this superiority would come to bear not only on the number of soldiers but on the industrial reserve capacity.

In economic capacity, the NATO states are nearly four times

superior to the Warsaw Pact nations (calculated at the official exchange rate). Who would dare want to wage war against nations with such great industrial superiority? And because the Warsaw Pact states' supply of goods lags far behind that of the Western industrialized nations qualitatively, is very frequently subject to shortfall, and often cannot be serviced and repaired (at least not without delay due to a lack of replacement parts), further sizable adjustments have to be made in the Eastern bloc. Scholars estimate the weighted economic strength of the Warsaw Pact states as one to seven vis-à-vis the NATO states. And Soviet leader Mikhail Gorbachev will have his hands full preventing the overall balance of power, which in the end always becomes the decisive factor in military effectiveness, from further deteriorating to the detriment of the Eastern bloc. Today Japan alone annually produces as much the equivalent of the gross national product of the Soviet Union.

Though surely not insignificant, economic and technological strength still can only provide the background for a comparison of military strengths. For centuries Prussia was an almost destitute state that fielded an army three times as large as any of the other European states. Yet heavy subsidies, occasionally French, occasionally British, were necessary to enable Prussia to rise at least temporarily into the concert of European powers. During World War II the Soviet Union had a comparable partner in the United States. Today, relying largely on itself, the Soviet Union confronts not only the United States and Western Europe but also China.

Neither in a protracted conventional war nor in a blitzkrieg can the Warsaw Pact impose its will on the West. From the Soviet standpoint, starting an unprovoked world war against such concerted strength as that of all the Western industrialized nations with any expectation of success is unthinkable. An exception might be to strike NATO with all the military might that is stationed in Eastern Europe in a kind of standing-start blitzkrieg, but this is not likely. In a longer lasting conventional war of attrition, the Soviet Union, supported solely by the East European states, has no chance of success because it would not be able permanently, or to any significant extent, to cut off supplies and reinforcements from the United States to Europe. Despite the Soviet Union's mighty efforts after World War II to create a global fleet out of thin air, the results have been negligible. NATO is superior to the Warsaw Pact in warships over 1,000 gross tons by a 2 to 1 ratio, in aircraft carriers by 7 to 1, in amphibious landing capacity by 5 to 1, and in marines by 14 to 1.[1] The slight inferiority in submarine fleets is more than compensated for by the geographic disadvantages of the Soviet Union with its easily blocked accesses to the high seas, the low performance levels of its ships, and the considerable advantage of Western anti-submarine warfare (ASW). Added to that is an inadequate system of bases. Today the Soviet Navy poses a problem for Western fleets, but one that could be controlled in a reasonable amount of time in the event of war.

The Soviet Union would likewise be hard put to sustain a standing-start blitzkrieg designed to produce shock and submission. While 4.8 million Soviets in military uniform is indeed impressive,[2] if we compare these soldiers by their functions with the corresponding forces in the West, a considerably less dramatic picture emerges. For example, just under one million soldiers are needed for the Strategic Rocket Forces of the Soviet Union, whereas the United States employs no more than 100,000 men to perform the same task. Where the Soviet Union uses 500,000 men for its coast guard and internal security, the United States gets by with about 100,000. Finally, a good 700,000 Soviet soldiers are utilized as cheap, untrained labor on construction sites, in agriculture, and for rail transport, while there is no comparable use of soldiers in the West.[3] In addition, one must also deduct something on the order of 600,000 troops stationed along the Chinese border, troops that could scarcely be spared for a conflict with NATO. Once we discount all this overmanning and

---

[1] *Annual Report to the Congress of Secretary of Defense Harold Brown for Fiscal Year 1982*, Washington, D.C.: GPO, 1981.

[2] *The Military Balance 1983–1984*, London: International Institute for Strategic Studies, 1983.

[3] Les Aspin, "Number Games Magnify Red Horde," *The Washington Star*, April 3, 1976; and Philip Morrison and Paul F. Walker, "A New Strategy for Military Spending," *Scientific American*, vol. 239, p. 52.

mismanning that poses little military threat to NATO, then we arrive at quite manageable figures.[4]

Based on current deployments, without longer warning times for both sides, the Soviet Union could attack only with its units stationed in the G.D.R. and Czechoslovakia. NATO must be and is able to deal with these units without further ado. If, in preparing an attack, the Soviets move their divisions stationed in the western military districts of the U.S.S.R. into the G.D.R. via the Polish rail and road system, then they will no longer be able to maintain the element of surprise. With few exceptions these divisions already require the addition of substantial numbers of reservists who would have to be drawn out of industry and subjected to an intensive refresher training. The mobilization and transportation of these units could not be kept secret, and so NATO would have adequate warning time.

For the West, potentially dangerous numbers of Warsaw Pact land forces are significant only when the armed forces of Eastern Europe are taken into account as an integral part of the attacking forces. In view of the experience of the last world war there is not the slightest inclination among the communist nations of Eastern Europe to enter into armed conflict. What could possibly induce a Pole, for example, to support actively a war for the Soviet Union? How could the Polish leadership get the followers of Solidarity to fight with their own blood for the extension of the hated Russian system into Western Europe? What is supposed to induce the devout Catholics of Poland to do this?

In fact, if the Soviet Union were to pursue such an adventuristic policy, it would be forced to exert even greater control over the East European nations by strengthening its occupation forces. Although they constitute the largest available body in Eastern Europe for an attack on the West, even the Soviet troops in East Germany could not be freed from occupation duties in the event of an offensive war against the West. And does anyone

---

[4]A rather well-balanced, overall picture of the global force ratio between East and West can be found in Admiral Antoine Sanguinetti, "La Désinformation sur la balance des forces: Armements et rapports de force," in *Cahiers du Forum pour l'indépendance et la paix*, no. 1, Summer 1983.

seriously believe that matters would be very different with respect to the Czechoslovakian forces? To be sure, the East German troops of the National People's Army are well trained and disciplined. But can a leadership in Moscow seriously believe that these forces could be deployed westward without problems, without there arising massive absenteeism, forms of passive resistance or even wholesale defections of units? None of the East European nations has accepted communism by a majority in free elections. It is known inside and outside the communist parties that the communist experiment on the Moscow model is no longer tenable. All the Eastern nations are attempting to raise loans in the West, reorient their foreign policies, and gain openings for self-determination.

Warning time for the West is measured in months, not hours, as NATO would have us believe. Unlike the Soviet troops in the G.D.R., the East European forces are not fully operational-ready without calling up reserves. And, as mentioned above, this process of calling up and drilling reservists would furnish the West with sufficient indication of impending hostilities. Years of intensive preparation would precede a world war, especially in light of the unequal distribution of economic strength between East and West. The purely military warning time would have to be measured in months at least if we add up all the inevitably recognizable indicators of war preparations in the Soviet Union and especially in its Western glacis. All the alarm that NATO has built up can only be explained as hysteria; it is not the product of a sober analysis of the East-West situation.

The alleged three-to-one matériel superiority of the East. Now, there is a wealth of official statistics that attribute a threefold or fourfold matériel superiority to the Soviets. Regarding naval forces, noted above, this is surely not the case. On the contrary, the West enjoys clear superiority in this realm, which it also needs more than the Soviet Union, which relies on land connections to a greater degree. But even in the case of conventional air forces this picture is not accurate if we add up not only the inventory of the European allies with U.S. matériel based in

Europe but include as well the worldwide, rapidly deployable forces outside Europe.

The U.S.S.R. would have taken leave of its senses if it were to look only at the Central European potential and not at global reinforcement possibilities. According to figures released by U.S. Senator Carl Levin, the balance of forces between NATO and the Warsaw Pact looks as follows: in the realm of medium-range bombers and ground attack aircraft the balance is 5,100 to 3,500; in strategic air transport, 316 to 225; in tactical air transport, 523 to 375; in air fueling, which is important for use of air fleets worldwide, 626 to 60; in air surveillance, 44 to 9; in carrier-based aircraft, 720 to 65; and in land-based ASW aircraft, 450 to 179—all in favor of the West.[5] These figures are surely not undisputed.

Nevertheless, all in all the picture seems anything but alarming for the West. This is particularly true when we take into account the much greater payload of Western aircraft, which can generally take on five to eight times that of their rival models in the East.[6] This allows for longer staying time in the air, more continuous sea and land surveillance, and greater payload of weapons, while reducing the fuel consumption needed to reach targets. The objection that aircraft stationed around the globe could not be assembled in a short space of time because of inadequate infrastructure can be accepted only in part. When France withdrew from the integrated military command, NATO lost a great many airfields with corresponding infrastructure. In the event of a large-scale attack by the Soviet Union on Western Europe, however, France will undoubtedly meet its Alliance commitments. Should European solidarity no longer serve as a basis for planning, then this would gravely undermine the ability of the Federal Republic and its Bundeswehr to withstand at-

---

[5]Carl Levin, *The Other Side of the Story: Some Military Advantages of the United States and our Allies over the U.S.S.R. and the Warsaw Pact,* May 1983. Based on Department of Defense and Defense Intelligence Agency data through December 31, 1982.

[6]Compare statistics in John M. Collins, *U.S.-Soviet Military Balance: Concepts and Capabilities, 1960–1980,* New York: McGraw-Hill, 1980, pp. 491–496.

tack. Nothing indicates such a danger. On the contrary, France is clearly making an effort to gear its security policy toward Europe.

At first glance there also appears to be a massive imbalance in the armaments of ground forces. Here again, taking into account global levels, we usually find a supposed three-to-one superiority of the East. It is doubtful, though, whether these figures should be taken at face value. Unlike the Western armies, which consider the costs of maintaining matériel, the Soviet army does not eliminate obsolete matériel but rather stores it in large depots for a contingency. Such obsolete arms are included in Western estimates of Warsaw Pact armaments. What amount of this equipment has already become unusable, and what is held in reserve for want of reliable repair is beyond the West's knowledge. The considerable number of breakdowns in machinery to which the Soviet economy is accustomed will presumably play a role with respect to the armed forces as well. The fact that Soviet recruits are generally trained on old equipment while newer arms are conserved, speaks for itself. In the West no one would think of training crews on a more than 20-year-old M–47 in order to send them into action in the M–1 or the Leopard II in wartime. Still, the accumulation of artillery and tank guns in the Eastern arsenals is considerable.

The West must keep these masses at bay; but it need not tremble. Several times Eastern matériel has had to face the test in armed conflicts between the Soviet-equipped Arab forces and, in terms of manpower and quantities of armaments, the always distinctly inferior Israeli troops. Even if we take into account that the latest technology may not always have been supplied, still it is out of the question to think that bad tank motors, bad hydraulics, fire-prone metal alloys, humanly unsupportable conditions in tank interiors, miserable clutches, etc., were intentionally delivered abroad. The conscript soldier in the Red Army, and not just Egyptians and Syrians, must deal with these very deficiencies. Thanks to the vehicles captured in all the Middle East campaigns, the U.S. Army has an excellent general idea of the deficiencies of the Soviet's weapons systems. The captured hardware reveals the very limited technological standards of the

Soviet Union's overall economic system, which the subsystem of weapons production simply cannot get around. In the case of tanks, even the latest models cannot hold a candle to the West's most effective modern tanks. This applies to virtually all aspects, from engine efficiency to the speed of range finding, the turning of the turret, etc. The experience with Soviet airplanes in various armed conflicts has by no means demonstrated the superiority or even equality of Soviet matériel. During the early stages of the Israeli invasion of Lebanon in the summer of 1982, the Israeli air force was able to shoot down 100 aircraft from about 300 sorties made by the Syrian Air Force, without any losses of their own. This was despite the fact that the Israeli pilots were not authorized to extend pursuit into Syrian territory, from where the enemy planes had taken off.

The age of the tank as the main weapon of attack is drawing to a close. Thanks to the variety of now very much more effective defensive weapons, use of the tank as an offensive weapons system calls for the utmost discretion. Formerly, for want of adequately effective anti-tank weapons for infantrymen, armored units that had broken through defense lines studded with anti-tank guns encountered scarcely any effective defense in depth. But today the situation is quite different. In a duel with a defending tank firing from cover, the attacking tank, which must leave its cover and therefore usually deliver not the first but, at best, the second shot, has a chance of survival of two to, at most, eight percent. Moreover, the attacking tank has to contend with anti-tank missiles shouldered by infantry, which it can handle only when it is able to neutralize those shooting the defensive missiles by direct fire. However, this will succeed only when it and accompanying tanks, operating in tandem, are not attacked by a shower of missiles at once. Add to this situation anti-tank mines of the third generation, shot from artillery tubes, laid down by combat engineers or, before long, with standoff weapons from airplanes, and the whole costly business of tanks (German predilection notwithstanding), will no doubt finally lose the battle against new tactical concepts. In his memoirs former Soviet leader Nikita S. Khrushchev had already grasped this instinctively when he wrote about observing maneuvers of Soviet army units: "When I arrived at the exercise area and saw how the tanks attacked and were put out of action in no time by anti-tank missiles, I felt sick. After all we are spending a lot of money to build tanks, but if—God forbid, as they say—a war breaks out, these tanks will get burnt out before they have reached the line to which the high command ordered them."[7]

In short, there is no cause for hysteria and frantic Western efforts. Anyone who argues for strengthening conventional defense by making extensive use of the new possibilities presented by emerging technologies must know that upon serious reflection the job certainly does not call for miracles. A decisive factor will be prudent selection of weapons and munitions that are feasible today and in some cases already on the market. The whole project need not and should not lead to a new, enormous armaments program. Rather, the West should progress at a calm, deliberate pace to cover longer time periods. This is all the more reasonable since even the CIA has now come to assess the real growth in Soviet arms spending in the 1970s at two percent, down from the earlier wild assessment of four percent. This growth falls in the range that, for example, the Federal Republic of Germany showed for the same period.

II. Strengthening Conventional Defense and Raising the Nuclear Threshold

Bound up with the emerging technologies are hopes of getting away from the presumably terrifying conventional inferiority of the West and its attendant doctrine of unavoidable and early-first-use of nuclear weapons. I regard the conventional inferior-

---

[7] Andrew Cockburn, *The Threat: Inside the Soviet Military Machine*, New York, Random House, 1983, p. 109.

ity of the West, all things considered, as by no means so marked as Western doctrine would have it. Thus, European security should in no way have to be so dependent on the first-use of nuclear weapons.

Eliminating battlefield nuclear weapons. Today there are still serious problems with tactical battlefield weapons, especially those that can be fired from artillery at a range of about 30 km. This tube artillery is suited to both nuclear and conventional warfighting. In practice this means that when a unit initially fighting by conventional means is threatened by a breakthrough from enemy forces, one must consider in timely fashion the artillery use of nuclear weapons. But a first-use of nuclear weapons could entail a response in kind from the Warsaw Pact in a matter of minutes. This consideration alone greatly diminishes the military attractiveness of tactical nuclear weapons.

Moreover, the process of political release of nuclear weapons results in serious difficulties. The military unit fighting with conventional means must reserve for nuclear operations artillery it would then lack in the conventional battle. The nuclear munitions must not be stored and guarded at too great a distance from the unit. Matériel stored near the front, however, is always in danger of being overrun. This in turn means that the military commander has to be inclined, by the "use them or lose them" principle, to support what could be a premature action to cross the nuclear threshold. Because presumably he knows the complicated political procedures for release of nuclear weapons, he must give thought well in advance to the course of his decision. Rather than deciding from an assessment of the immediate situation, he must estimate what the course of events will be in the next 48 hours and propose release for such conditions. The various battlefield problems that the corps commander has could be resolved by a general release procedure for tactical nuclear weapons that delegates the authority to decide to him. But this the Federal Republic cannot allow, because extended combat with nuclear battlefield weapons on West German soil would destroy the greatest part of what is actually supposed to be defended. Any West German government will therefore permit at most only a very selective use of nuclear battlefield weapons and must oppose any general release. For such reasons, but also because of the fear of losing control over escalation once the nuclear threshold is crossed, military and political logic calls for giving up virtually all of this type of nuclear armaments. Battlefield nuclear weapons, including the neutron bomb, should be replaced with conventional means. This would raise the nuclear threshold. As replacement for the eliminated battlefield nuclear weapons, large numbers of anti-tank weapons of the most varied technologies must be procured, and these must be capable of preventing any breakthrough by tank concentrations.

Conventionalizing the mission of NATO's air forces. Nuclear deep-strike operations with air forces pose another problem. Because the air defense of Western Europe is anything but sufficient, NATO finds itself compelled, upon the outbreak of a war, to initiate immediate deep-strike attacks and destroy the enemy air force on the ground, particularly their airfields, so as to reduce drastically the other side's sortie rates and ultimately to gain an air superiority. The same applies to operations to counter Warsaw Pact ground reinforcements by bringing up the second echelon out of the western military districts of the Soviet Union via the rail systems of Poland and the G.D.R. Until now the means available for carrying out such actions have been essentially nuclear. The use of these nuclear weapons is extremely problematic, because the other side now has similarly devastating weapons at its disposal, which it will certainly employ as a countermeasure in the event of Western first use. The total destruction of the battlefield, and that would probably be, in effect, the entire Federal Republic of Germany and on the other side the German Democratic Republic, hardly makes this form of warfighting attractive to the Germans. The Germans have never devoted particular attention to the question of what will happen to them if deterrence fails. Given the horrors of the answer, the question was simply repressed, while refuge was sought in the abstract political dogmas of deterrence doctrine. This has now changed as a result of the Pershing II debate. Now that the questions have been raised one looks for remedies through conventional arms. Interest in finding a solution to nuclear dilemmas through conventional defense should be great for the United States as well since it wants to avoid the lurking danger of escalation that could end in an intercontinental exchange.

The danger of conventional "pushbutton" wars. In conventionalizing targets that were previously reserved for theater nuclear forces we are, in effect, raising a number of serious questions about military stability between the two blocs. The strong inhibitions on both sides about crossing the nuclear threshold, be it only at the tactical level, have in the past obstructed our view of problems that could increasingly lead to conventional pushbutton wars of lightning speed. Conventionalizing what were previously operations for nuclear weapons can lead to combat situations that promise victory to the side that strikes first. Just as the West is not prepared to believe the Soviet Union's longstanding assurances that the U.S.S.R. has no intention of attacking the West, so too are the Soviets hard put to believe in the West's unmitigated love of peace or indeed its discinclination to wage an offensive war against Eastern Europe. Both czarist Russia and the Soviet Union have had their historical experience with Western nations. The military campaigns of the Swedes, the French, the Germans against Russia are all still remembered. From time to time Western nations have been interested in alliances with the Soviet Union for specific purposes, such as defeating Hitler's Germany. But ever since 1917 they have found it difficult to recognize a communist social order's right to exist. So just as we in the West scrutinize Soviet armaments for their potential use in an offensive war and trouble ourselves little over Moscow's peaceful declarations, this naturally is what the other side is doing as well.

A conventional disarming strike against air forces, command centers, and supply junctions within minutes is becoming conceivable. If we consider the spectrum of future weapons and munitions that emerging technologies make possible, the Soviet Union has reason to be anxious about the technological prowess of the West. A few high-precision hits on railroad bridges and switching areas, etc., using conventional smart weapons could sever the lifelines of the Soviets' first defense ring in Eastern Europe. The 19 elite divisions in East Germany would then be left without reinforcements and supplies. The matériel from the depots in Poland would not come through. A major part of the aircraft on the ground could be hit in or outside of shelters and neutralized with a surprise attack. The runways could be destroyed and time mines could delay their restoration. Alternate airfields have no shelter protection. Plus the limited ranges and technological backwardness of the aircraft relative to Western models would put the Soviet Union at a further disadvantage. Moreover, within the shortest space of time the command centers required for waging conventional warfare could be put out of action by missiles, cruise missiles, or airplanes. This means that within minutes rather than hours the Soviet troops in Eastern Europe would be left without central command. And the emergence of popular uprisings, which are apt to tie down the Soviet forces in internal struggles, would then pose the gravest danger of all in Soviet eyes. This might be one terror scenario for the Soviet military.

Clearly, the East will not rest until it has armed itself with comparable emerging technology capabilities in the military realm. This goal can be achieved in five to ten years at the latest. By that time we will have a highly unstable situation on both sides, in the conventional as well as the nuclear realm. Whichever side acts with sufficient force and resolution could very quickly put the other in a position from which it will be difficult to extricate itself.

If we play this game through from East to West rather than West to East, we come up with more than unpleasant consequences for the West. On the assumption that the East attacks with weapons of the emerging technologies class just described, then within minutes the communications network that, for example, links the West's tactical nuclear weapons with the political leadership of the United States would be put out of action. The AWACS (Airborne Warning and Control System) bases would be unusable. The NATO pipeline system would be destroyed for a long time. The operational bases of NATO air forces would be rendered useless. Rail junctions for moving up Belgian and Dutch troops would be destroyed. The supply areas for the U.S. Rapid Deployment Forces would be rendered unserviceable. NATO's conventional combat units in the Federal Republic would face tremendous deployment problems; their command centers would largely be paralyzed. There would be very limited potential for reconnaissance by means of aircraft or even reconnaissance drones. Within a few minutes or hours, the initial loss in combat strength would be irreplaceable.

Naturally the West would then in a further round of arms acquisition spare no effort at making the "Follow-on Forces Attack" (FOFA) weapons survivable against a preemptive strike by the East. This could allow NATO to try to cripple the adversary in a fashion similar to the one described just above. The threat to use nuclear weapons would then have little persuasive power, as the other side could at once initiate commensurate countermeasures.

The road to conventional pushbutton war is becoming irresistible. The danger of the new technologies is that they could reinforce the trend whereby the one who strikes first could gain enormous advantages that his opponent could no longer offset. How long over the decades can mankind rely on the strength of nerve of leaders on both sides to resist the temptation to let fly? This is not just a question to the totalitarian regimes of the East; it also applies to the states of the Western Alliance. Are the democratic systems of government really so completely immune to irrational decisions? In the past the psychologically significant threshold of a nuclear holocaust has helped to check acts of folly. Yet with modern conventional weapons fired from a seemingly secure hinterland, the West may begin to allow itself a certain degree of carelessness in using these new blitzkrieg weapons. The escalatory effect of such weapons should not be underestimated. The conventional defense capability of a superpower or its alliance could soon be at stake. Very quickly a superpower could be left impotent—a situation it must avoid at all costs. For this reason it might waste no time in escalating by striking at new targets, or in desperation it might finally threaten to use atomic weapons. Thus the nuclear threshold could be, not raised, but inescapably lowered by modern technologies used by one side to debilitate an adversary by lightning-fast conventional means.

It is strikingly apparent that we find ourselves in danger of racing toward a partially or fully automated battlefield. The race to perfect systems with new pushbutton technologies appears unstoppable. Even if it is decided not to pursue such armaments for fear of destabilizing the East-West military balance, no one can be sure that the other side has not long ago set out on this road. One, therefore, has to keep up. Thus it is assured that the arms race will continue for years to come. There may be a will for détente, but the forces of circumstance drive the military men and politicians in a different direction. Lack of dialogue between West and East makes it easy for the propagandists on both sides. Easier anyway than if efforts were begun to organize, at least in Europe, a world that, though it may suffer from tensions, can no longer be blown up through military adventures.

A new security philosophy. Are there ways now that would enable the West, perhaps jointly or in coordination with the East, to extricate itself from these dangers and absurdities? Naturally we can try by way of negotiations on arms control and disarmament to guard against the greatest dangers of destabilizing weapons. Experience in Vienna and Geneva, however, does not leave one optimistic. These negotiations must encompass too many incomparable parameters for them to avoid falling prey to the various lobbies and hawks eager for weapons procurement. In the end such negotiations can yield something only when there are statesmen at work on both sides who are capable and willing to take action and who see through the systemic problems. But the statistical probability of this happening is not high, so we should not entertain very great hopes.

Are there, however, defense structures that might be realized, in part unilaterally, in part by East-West accord, to offer security and help escape the arms race? Looking at the protracted struggle first in Korea, then in Vietnam, but also considering the Soviets' battles with the Afghan rebels, we see that even today the industrialized nations' most refined technology, optimized over decades for wars in Europe, can be put out of operation with simple and primitive methods. Where then, outside of Europe and the sparsely covered Middle East, which is strongly influenced by European war experience, can battles still be waged on the Central European model? In other parts of the world a determined resistance force that relies on the population, that can dissolve into it, and that is adequately equipped with anti-tank and anti-helicopter weapons will be able to make life miserable for an occupation of intervention forces from the highly technological North. Of course, Vietnam and Afghanistan can be no more than indicative. The incomparability of initial conditions relative to Europe makes simulation impossible. Yet the question must be allowed whether from the experience of two world wars the highly technological nations of the North have not become stuck in a dead-end street where they are trapped by their own cemented ways of thinking, simple follow-on planning, fascination with technology, and vested interests.

More stable defensive structures. The Europeans and particularly the Germans no longer have any desire to organize or even countenance any sort of war on their territory. This raises the question whether entirely different structures from the present ones would not be appreciably better suited to defensive combat in Central Europe. In the 1950s, to safeguard Western Europe against the suspected aggression from the Soviet Union, the United States wanted to immediately endow the full 500,000-man Budeswehr, with the fighting quality of the German Wehrmacht. Evidently there was no inclination on the German side at the time to give greater consideration to a different structure better suited to a future European order of peace.

Today in Europe alternatives to NATO's current type of defense are found in the small neutral countries of Sweden and Switzerland, and with some qualifications also in Austria. The armies of Switzerland and Sweden were not involved in the battles of the World War II. After the war's end they were arrogantly and somewhat superficially dismissed as lacking the necessary experience in battle with potential Eastern aggressors. It was little noted that for decades these nations had geared their substantial military efforts exclusively for defense, while the basic structures in West and East arose more from the offensive structures of the World War II. The Bundeswehr was profoundly marked by the experience of the Wehrmacht, especially in its campaign against the Soviet Union. The Wehrmacht, however, had been consciously armed for offensive war with a structure that relied on the tank as its main weapon. Later it was forced to employ its optimal offensive instrument, the tank, for defensive purposes. Of course something quite similar is true of the Soviet army. The basic models for the postwar combat units were not the structures that had stood the test in the defensive battle for Moscow but rather those that had proved themselves in the offensive battles from the winter of 1943 on. Thus in West and East we are faced with units and combat structures that are optimally designed for offensive assault.

The Swiss and Swedish examples. A look at the Swedish and Swiss structures strikingly shows that these certainly not militarily incompetent nations put a considerable emphasis on the infantry. Their defense is organized on a very much more static, area-covering basis. Since both nations have never wanted anything else but to defend themselves, their defense is less schematic and very much adapted to their terrains. Both countries are in a position to cultivate, maintain, and make use of the defense readiness of their populations. In so doing they utilize the strength of a large portion of the male population. In part because of their geographic circumstances they do not have very much recourse to in-place units manned by 18-year-olds, but rely very heavily on well-trained reserves, even in their command structures. Their term of military service is limited to the time required for training the simple recruit. In Sweden this is seven months. Noncommissioned officers and officers of the reserve are trained longer but do receive a remuneration in this period. For the time of their active military service the soldiers remain with their respective units, which are trained at regular intervals. These units are heavily equipped with defensive weapons against tanks and airplanes. There is less reliance on a defensive cordon as in the case of NATO strategy, but rather on an area-covering defense. Hence, a penetrating, low-flying combat aircraft can be engaged also by infantry defensive forces in the hinterland. There are indeed tanks and armored infantry fighting vehicles because only such weapons systems enable one to recapture lost territory. But it cannot be said that, as with the armies of NATO, particularly the Bundeswehr, the tank is regarded as the primary means of combatting the tank.

For their defense the Swiss and the Swedes have thus set up relatively tight-knit configurations in order to stop attacking, highly mechanized units; behind these stand defense forces with strong tank components that can be used at points of main effort where there is a danger of breakthrough. These forces are not sufficient, however, to be used for territory-taking offensive operations. In contrast, at the center of NATO's armament is the great mass of tanks that can not only be used at the points of main effort in the defensive battle (which would be sensible from a cost-effectiveness standpoint) but are also designated for a kind of cordon defense along the intra-German border. Behind this cordon there are scarcely any reserves to speak of, except for a small, barely trained infantry anti-tank capacity.

"Deep strike" and the lightning kill. In combat against attacking aircraft formations, the NATO strategy looks quite similar. In contrast to Sweden, air defense in depth is as yet practically nonexistent. It is hoped that penetrating combat aircraft can be intercepted by Hawk and the now being installed Patriot anti-aircraft missiles, which are replacing the outdated Nike system. If breaches are made in this cordon, the gaps can be filled only by the very costly use of fighter aircraft. Ports, traffic junctions, airports, etc., have no appreciable air defense capability at their disposal. Because of the high cost of the NATO air defense cordon, investment in air defense in depth is presumably out of the question.

This, however, has far-reaching consequences for NATO strategy. In the belief that one cannot rely solely on the air defense cordon to hold off an attack, the combined air forces of NATO are planning an attack on the Warsaw Pact's operational airfields in the G.D.R. and Poland immediately following the outbreak of hostilities in order either to destroy the enemy air forces on the ground or else reduce their operational capability by putting their home bases out of action. Both sides have these deep interdiction capabilities—whether they are for purposes of defense or for attack right from the start is beside the point. Again we see the essentially unwanted effect that the one who attacks with lightning speed gains inordinate advantages, while the one who strikes second faces irrecoverable disadvantages. The pressure to launch a preemptive strike thus seems ineluctable. If the East were able to neutralize the NATO air defense cordon at least in a few flight paths, or if in the future it were able to fly around the cordon with more efficient aircraft, then a large part of the NATO infrastructure would lie unprotected against enemy air attacks. Conversely, from the Eastern standpoint, if NATO launches a surprise, lightning-fast air attack on the East's air bases, then the Warsaw Pact can within hours be deprived of air supremacy over its own territory. Because of existing armaments, vulnerabilities and strategies both sides are practically forced to go for the jugular within minutes in order to assure a more-or-less adequate chance of survival. The scenario is that of a knife fight. Fractions of seconds in stabbing decide the survival of one side or the other. Lightning-fast action is rewarded with triumph. He who hesitates is lost.

A strategy of defensive entanglement. The opposite scenario from a lightening kill would subject the aggressor to a sustained bloodletting that would increase with the intensity of his attack. Every offensive action would result in the greatest possible attrition of the attacking forces. The aggressor would bleed to death in the defensive tangle while the side being attacked would maintain second-strike forces in reserve. The defender could use these resources to inflict the decisive decimating strike after attrition and, in any case, to effectively stop units that had broken through. This strategy of avoiding the decisive battle and instead trying to subject the attacking forces to severe attrition is certainly not new; it is as old as military history itself.

Implementing such a strategy would mean discarding, for one thing, the operational plans of NATO air forces. Air defense would have to be structured more for covering specific territories and in conformity with the objects to be protected. In addition, there would have to be, based on the Swedish model, a drastic reduction of the ground targets that are at all rewarding for an opponent. Providing the ground defense with relatively cheap weapons to defend against low-flying aircraft would drive the expensive ground attack aircraft to higher altitudes. These in turn could and necessarily would fall prey to anti-tank missiles.

Whatever survived would have to be either put up with or destroyed in aircraft-to-aircraft combat with standoff weapons as much as possible. Perhaps air mines, yet to be developed, could also force enemy combat aircraft up to higher altitudes.

It seems remarkable to me that there are ideas and research initiatives for destroying missiles in flight, but that to this day NATO has not managed to develop a procurement-ready, accurate, air-based, anti-aircraft weapon of intermediate range. Since the air forces of virtually all nations are led by pilots, the supporters of manned flying, a major share of defense funds is again and again lavished on perfecting the airplane. Defensive weapons and munitions often lag markedly behind aircraft development. However, airplanes have meanwhile become so expensive that for cost considerations alone they ought perhaps to assume the role of roving systems that serve as a backup in situations that become extremely dangerous.

Central European terrain and anti-tank defense. If we look at the military aspect of geography in the defense landscape between East and West in Europe, we realize very quickly that the terrain, especially in Germany, is anything but favorable for tanks on either side of the borders. The old gate of entry from the south out of Hungary over Lower Austria to Lower Bavaria opens on Austrian territory, which is adverse for tanks, since the terrain can be defended easily, provided the Austrian forces move to defend. This line of attack would entail immense deployment problems for the Soviet Union, for with the four divisions stationed in Hungary it could in no way launch a standing attack. An invasion from Czechoslovakia, where five Soviet divisions have been deployed since 1968, would have to be carried out over the Bohemian Forest and the Bavarian Forest up to the Fichtel Gebirge, mountainous regions that are poorly, or not at all, suited for tanks. The offensive planners would have to take into account that a more or less intelligently waged defense would ensnare thousands and thousands of tanks at fords, on steep slopes, in narrow corridors and roads, and in between wooded areas.

The contiguous Thuringian Forest, the Rhone, and the Harz likewise provide passageways little suited for tanks. The famous

"Fulda Gap," the largest westward bulge in the G.D.R. border, appears attractive to the Soviets as a gate of entry on maps that do not show the terrain relief. In reality, especially on the G.D.R. side, the Thuringian Forest presents a natural obstacle with very few passageways. And these can be easily blocked by the West. North of the Harz there are a few broad tracts that might be suitable for tank breakthroughs, but not for thousands and thousands of tanks advancing all at the same time. The terrain up to the Baltic is by no means as consistently favorable for tanks as is often depicted. Heath and moorlands, woodlands, rivers and canals afford convenient obstacles. Plus a cultivated landscape of fields and meadows surrounded by hedges, which, together with frequently interspersed smaller woods, provides cover for a geographically informed anti-tank defense.

Backed by the Baltic Sea, the Lauenburg lake district also forms an obstacle to tanks. If the Red Army, together with its less reliable satellite armies really wanted to engage its tank arsenals effectively, it would have to concentrate the tanks again and again on narrow routes of advance and these would offer optimal targets to an active anti-tank defense. In this case the highly intelligent, third-generation, anti-tank weapons would provide an excellent means to immobilize the enemy. The enormous spread of low-density settlements, even urbanization of large parts of the borderlands over the past 40 years, has created further large impediments. Their use as potential cover for anti-tank warfare is viewed with mixed feelings by the local population and is thus very controversial. All the same, the other side cannot assume that it will get free passage here.

For a conventional attack on Norway and neutral Sweden, the tank weapon is hardly feasible. Here instead we would probably have to consider the threat of airborne landings designed to take key areas, especially ports and airports. The primary means of defense against these would again be static defense systems. Extensive tank armies are not necessary. Nor does either country have them. To the south of the Federal Republic the Alps form a protective barrier against tanks, where a reasonably effectively organized defense would have to be conducted more by infantry. The nearby Adriatic forms a barrier to any conventional land battle. At most one might fear a breakthrough into the Po Valley.

But the extremely dense settlement and urbanization of the Po Valley make it problematic for heavily mechanized units to advance and provide the defender with various possibilities for putting up resistance. The border area between the Soviet Union and Turkey also tends to favor anti-tank defense over tank warfare. Thus if we want to get away from the present Janus-faced defense structure in Europe, we might find, in conjunction with the new weapons technologies emerging over the coming decades, a geography that is optimal for defense, especially for those allies situated on the bloc frontiers.

Foregoing destabilizing offensive weapons. Now, if we attempt to put into effect the principle that the one who attacks loses more forces the deeper his attack advances—i.e., he tends to bleed to death—then we should consciously depart from the knife-fight scenarios with their lightning breakthroughs and ability to cut through whole defense systems. Strategies and weapons established for such missions should be dismantled. Wherever security permits, the West should forego development and procurement of destabilizing weapons. NATO and the Bundeswehr both claim to be so lightly armed that there could be no question of offensive potential. Mention has been made of the limited logistic capabilities of NATO and the Bundeswehr, and also of the inadequate medical care for advancing troops. Apart from the fact that these capabilities can be readily reestablished it must also be borne in mind that the Soviet Union certainly cannot feel as secure, as is always assumed in the West. All things considered, the full spectrum of risk for the East is at least as great as that for the West. This would apply all the more if NATO were to procure conventional weapons that could selectively and suddenly eliminate the command and control capability of Soviet troops in Eastern Europe.

In the area of army weaponry we ought to reduce the number of tanks. We could also reduce the quantity of such anti-aircraft artillery as the Gepard that have become an indispensable and infinitely expensive means for defending the tank against air attacks. On the other hand, we ought to make further concerted efforts to strengthen anti-tank defense capability with various kinds of anti-tank weapons. These include, for example, mines of the third generation. These work at a distance of 50 meters, are not activated until the tank approaches, and can be programmed for the number of tanks coming. These mines can be hand laid by combat engineers, or they can be shot from rocket launchers with ranges from 2 to 70 km. and can thus immobilize approaching tanks while they are still concentrated. The multi-purpose Tornado can selectively scatter such mines.

It would be beyond the scope of this essay to go further into the details of weapons technology. But it seems to me that a sufficiently deeply layered line of defense organized in this way with modern anti-tank weapons would enable us to build a better conventional defense than that of the present tank-heavy, and hence very expensive, mechanized units, which offer no guarantee of being in the right place at the right time. Such a defense could be constructed so that it would offer no significant targets to either an enemy air force or enemy artillery. The more intensively the enemy attacks, the more he will bleed. He will wear out his best troops and his best matériel. Naturally the weapons must be constituted in such a way that they can be neither deceived nor readily put out of action. The anti-tank weapons available today have been extremely accurate in peacetime trials. Under conditions of combat, however, the operator of the precision weapon will often fall to enemy fire while tracking his target. For this reason too, it is essential to have a diversified network of defensive weapons. The anti-tank helicopter can be a help if it is used over one's own territory at points of main effort against penetrating tanks. In large numbers its use would be of very limited cost effectiveness because its vulnerability to enemy infantry fire is too high, and weapons will soon be available that can pose an even greater danger to the helicopter.

Eliminating the pressure for deep strike. It would then be important to consider whether we could get rid of the pressure to immediately destroy the other side's air bases and air force. Instead, one's own air force would have to be held back, perhaps even withdrawn, in order to deny the enemy points of attack. A well-distributed air defense would be needed to guarantee the wearing down of the enemy. High priority would have to be given to highly intelligent medium- and short-range air defense missiles. Should these weapons prove effective, the number of fighters could be kept relatively low, but with enough of course retained for emergencies. I doubt whether in the long run NATO's air defense cordon with its high costs for equipment and personnel is the appropriate response to the Eastern threat. NATO's air defense positions might one day be put out of action by means of such modern Eastern technology as ballistic or cruise missiles and would then scarcely be worth the money.

I would give the structures as much a decentralized configuration as possible and would rely on greater dispersal of reconnaissance means such as drones in order to dispense with central nerve centers, which would be extremely susceptible to enemy attacks or deceptions. Central battlefield management appears to me almost predestined to become the first deceived and blinded. On the other hand, I would be extremely hesitant to base my defense capability on NATO's attempt to neutralize the Warsaw Pact's command centers, from the battalion to the army level. This would again produce the disposition to pushbutton disarming strikes that immediately, and possibly uncontrollably, drive the opponent to the maximum escalation, as would indeed be the case if the situation were reversed. What are American troops supposed to do if "battlefield management systems" are neutralized and they are left without central command? There would remain only escalation to the first use of nuclear weapons, precisely the solution we must set out to avoid.

Conventional strikes against follow-on forces—the costs of FOFA. Similar considerations must be made in regard to the second- and third-echelon follow-on forces. Realization of Supreme Allied Commander Europe, General Bernard W. Rogers's ideas on combatting these forces would most likely come at the expense of the defense capability of the immediate front line. This in turn would give the Soviet Union a good reason to move up rapidly and interweave its second echelon with its first echelon so that the NATO follow-on forces would thrust into emptiness. The Soviets would then break through up front.

This issue is also vitally important because no FOFA mission into the enemy's hinterland can be carried out successfully without the very highest accuracy of munitions. Within a certain range this in turn presupposes a refinement in navigation that in the past has been built into airplanes and nuclear delivery vehicles only and that will be exceedingly expensive to implement. If the course of these conventional missiles and cruise missiles are to be directed by means of satellite navigation, it will become increasingly important to be the first to bring down the other side's satellites. Thus once again the knife-fight scenario would arise. Yet, if NATO does not adopt satellite mid-course correction, then navigation of conventional weapons alone will consume enormous sums. Missiles cannot be fired over hundreds of kilometers with such accuracy that the conventional payload can overcome deception tactics and still effectively deliver on target. Costs alone would practically rule out such a venture. If, however, NATO makes the defense network sufficiently strong and furnishes the potential to break the initial wave of combat forces, then it should be able to do so without General Rogers's concept of FOFA for the most part. At least it should not be exclusively dependent on FOFA. A certain disruption and cutting off of the avenues of advance must be desirable. However, this should not be expanded into a defense that stakes everything on the card of totally paralyzing the adversary's system.

Of course, a static defense also costs money, but savings are possible in the long run. A more defensively oriented defense calls for large numbers of weapons and soldiers. It cannot rely on concentrations that can be seized by the enemy's rapidly mobile units within the shortest space of time. The weapons systems in the kind of strategy I have advocated are cheaper per item than the tank-heavy defense, but the costs are not insignificant when the weapons and munitions are deployed over the terrain. At least this will be true of the transitional period until the defensive structure is in place. After that it could in fact become less expensive, especially in terms of operations and maintenance.

III. West German Defense Policy: A Critique

The Federal Republic will be able to maintain a balanced defense commitment in the 1990s only if military structures are radically changed. In the next decade Bonn will not be able, except at excessive cost, to find adequate manpower for its armed forces, nor will it be able to ensure sufficient armaments. For reasons of demographic development, the 1990s will see just 50 percent of the present draft-age cohort available for the Bundeswehr. Although today we have an oversupply of manpower from the years of high birth rates, the situation will have changed completely by the mid-1990s at the latest. Industry and the Bundeswehr will fight over the new generation, and it is scarcely conceivable that the public sector will be able to satisfy its demand without strong incentives. But the present policy of extending military service is heading in the wrong direction. While all other NATO countries have either abolished compulsory military service or drastically shortened it, the West German government thinks it has to go the opposite way. Young people, who today are extraordinarily well-trained in civilian professions, will be kept a few months longer in their barracks at a relatively lower level of motivation and at low pay, so as to be available within hours in the event of war. This does not make the armed forces more popular and it squanders money on the wrong item, money that will then be lacking for armaments and munitions.

At present the problems remain concealed behind a wealth of optimistic assumptions in the government's manpower and financial planning. But the West German government's planning for the 1990s works out only on paper. The sum total cannot possibly come out right. And because in our democracy two to four years has become the maximum time horizon, the consequences are going to hit the successors of the present government in Bonn. Mindful of any reaction from its allies—be it the United States as the buttress of West German security interests, be it our European neighbors who might well turn away and subscribe to a defense at the lowest possible cost to the detriment of all Western Europe—the West German government is not facing the basic problem that is fast approaching. Yet sometime by the end of the 1980s or at the latest in the 1990s the Federal Republic's increasingly incongruous defense contribution will have to be put on the agenda, nationally and in the Alliance. Long-term East-West political objectives could be one factor influencing the reorientation.

Reserves and the better use of reserve units. Irrespective of the future structure of the Bundeswehr, in the 1990s the Federal Republic will confront problems that can no longer be solved by applying today's policies. For example, the current structure overemphasizes standing forces and neglects the reserves. To obtain its sovereignty and admission to NATO the Federal Republic committed itself to field a military force of 495,000 troops. This goal was finally reached in the late 1970s. These 495,000 soldiers have at their disposal modern weapons in effective, highly mechanized units. In the event of tension or war the Bundeswehr can expand to about 1.3 million men. For full mobilization the units currently in place need an additional 200,000 men in order to become fully operational. This pertains primarily to personnel in logistics, medical care, traffic control, etc. The conscripts drawn in each year are trained exclusively for the standing army of 495,000. In many cases they receive arduous and very costly training in complicated and expensive weapons. Often it takes nearly a year to 15 months before the conscript can actually master the weapons system entrusted to him or his team. A commmander of the Leopard II tank will often not be able to use this 5.5 million-deutsche mark weapons system to full effect. At the end of 15 months the training is generally thrown away, as now a team of new recruits with no previous service take charge of the equipment. The whole process of training and systematic exercise begins anew. The tank commander or his gunner as well, following a 12-month transitional period in which he would be called back to his old unit in the event of war, is assigned to the reserves and thus to the so-called Territorial Army. There he will be called up again at the very most a few more times as a reservist, but he receives new duties, such as guarding militarily important infrastructure, for which he was not trained in his term of active duty. Nor as a rule does he know how to handle anti-tank weapons competently so as to combat an enemy tank that has broken through.

All this should be changed in the course of restructuring the Bundeswehr. The question of standing units must be reformulated. We ought to look not so much at how many men are kept in these units but rather at which defense functions can be performed by reserves and what has to be kept ready for a potential buildup in the event of tensions or war. Naturally this question is connected with what is militarily exploitable early warning time. As described above, this early warning time covers weeks and months and not just hours, as NATO planning presumes. In this case, then, we can fall back on reserves to a much greater extent than with the present structure.

A more static defense requires a great deal of manpower in case of war. This personnel, especially for a network that is strong on anti-tank defense, should by no means be manned by conscripts but rather, as in Sweden and Switzerland, by reserves. Here the population living near the border could be called upon as initial, immediately available, defense components. This population knows the terrain of its home area. During their period of active military service and later in reserve exercises, intensive training educates these soldiers in the military utilization of the terrain with the available weapons systems. Mine barriers could be expertly laid and monitored in the shortest space of time by forces familiar with the area. A large segment of the conscripts should be trained solely for these missions from the start. Another segment should be conscripted into the highly mechanized units presently in place. Like the allied NATO units, these units could be dedicated to the points of concentration in battle, to the enemy's main axes of attack. Outside the main lines of attack the defense in the border area rests essentially on the network sketched above. Since the Federal Republic cannot man simultaneously both standing units at their present levels and the militia-like defense network—and absolutely not if in the near future the low birth rate age-groups reduce conscription by nearly half—the highly mechanized, tank-heavy units will have to be in some instances restructured, in others dissolved over time.

While the Federal Republic today does make a contribution to NATO on the order of 495,000 troops in standing units, the growth goal to the targeted 1.3 million men in case of tensions is assured quantitatively but not qualitatively. If we are to reshape the Bundeswehr's structure and training system for rapid and qualitatively adequate realization of the 1.3 million-man defense force, then cuts have to be made in the standing forces. Whereas the United States has the great advantage of being far removed from the hostilities in the event of a conventional war, the Federal Republic has the inescapable disadvantage of directly becoming a battlefield in the first seconds of war. Conversely, the United States has the geographic disadvantage that it has long routes of advance to the potential battle area, whereas the West Germans live in the battle area itself. A third of the population in fact lives within a strip of 100 km. along the intra-German border. The male portion of this population could furnish the necessary troops for the more infantry-oriented interdiction network. For that we do not need any standing units languishing in their barracks. The traffic infrastructure of the Federal Republic is so outstanding that the cadre-strength units can be filled in a matter of hours. Even from the remotest areas of the Federal Republic the borderland can be reached in four to eight hours; in a more territorially conceived land and air defense, with positions more toward the middle of the country, it would be still faster. Such proposals should be discussed with our allies in an unbiased way. This would be more beneficial for NATO than muddling along in the cherished, but in the future no longer sustainable defense structures. Restructuring the Bundeswehr along the lines proposed would permit military service in West Germany to be reduced to a duration of seven or eight months by the 1990s.

Forward defense and the forces of the allies. One firm aspect of the Federal Republic's defense policy has to be emphasized once again: the West German interest in maintaining forward defense right at the intra-German border. Almost equally important, the Western defense line should be held on the border not only by West German troops but by the troops of all the allies. For deterrence is greatly enhanced simply by the fact that from the start of a war American, British, Dutch, Danish, Canadian and Belgian units would be involved immediately in the fighting. This still does have its political and psychological impact on East and West today. However, there would be absolutely no difficulty in placing the forward, static defense network to be filled essentially by West German reserves under the command of the respective NATO defense sectors. Because the highly mechanized mobile forces are stationed in and behind the network so as to be able to apply themselves to the points of concentration in the conflict, there do not appear, as some critics fear, to be tracts of purely national West German defense.

Yet one demand of West German defense policy in the Alliance remains indispensable. The defense must be waged with the greatest intensity on the intra-German border. Alternative defense proposals must not turn the entire Federal Republic into the battlefield of a modern conventional war. Hence, a more static defense concept must present substantial concentrations along the intra-German border in a strip of 50 to 75 km. If it appears that highly mechanized units can in all probability be prevented from getting through this strip, the other side will of its own accord abandon any idea of attacking. The deterrent effect is then ensured.

Would the transition from the highly mechanized units to static defense structures be a problem for the Alliance? Conflicts might ensue in the Alliance as a result of non-uniform, in fact dangerously diverging, structures. Yet upon closer examination there appears to be a convergence between some of the ideas considered here for the future of the Bundeswehr and what is being planned and carried out in both France and the United States in the way of tactical military development.

The American Rapid Deployment Forces, but also the U.S. Marine Corps with its 192,000 men, constitute units that are not outfitted with heavy equipment to the extent that is customary under Central European conditions. These troops can take with them only what can be rapidly loaded and transported in airplanes or in some cases landing craft. The Force d'Action Rapide recently instituted by the French also consists more than the regular French Army of strong anti-tank defense infantry, which is designated for action in the Mediterranean and Africa by way of helicopter or transport aircraft but could also be used in Europe. Such units could be readily integrated into the type of new defensive structure I have outlined.

For the rest we must take a sober look at the extremely high investment in tanks, armored infantry combat vehicles, and other heavy equipment now in place in Central Europe. With this hardware there is not all that much that can be done elsewhere around the globe. In the Third World, where conflicts often take the form of revolts organized from within the population, the

West's dependence on heavy weaponry, overburdened by technology and cost, becomes more of a trap than an advantage. All the more reason to abandon the blitzkrieg strategies of the Second World War that have become a dead-end street for the East and the West.

Withdrawing American and Soviet forces from Europe by the year 2000. The West should combine its long-term defense conceptions for Western Europe with new and bolder disarmament proposals. The Mutual and Balanced Force Reduction negotiations should be divested of their "alibi" function not only of preventing initiatives from the U.S. Congress for reducing U.S. forces in Europe but also of clinging to the present configuration of the Bundeswehr. Efforts should be made to at least induce the East European countries progressively to give up their World War II defense structures à la Guderian and de Gaulle. They could do this by reorganizing present units into a structure more geared to defense, as I have sketched here for the West.

The Soviet Union as a world power cannot be induced to transform its armed forces into a purely defensive structure as proposed for the West European and perhaps East European armies; but it can eliminate a sizable portion of the Warsaw Pact, particularly Soviet, standing units step-by-step as Western units are restructured. The Soviets should be taken at their word when they unofficially offer to pull 50 percent of the units stationed in Eastern Europe back to their homeland. In the G.D.R. there would then remain only 9 or at most 10 divisions directly confronting the West, instead of the present 19; in Czechoslovakia we would see only 2 or 3 divisions; and in Hungary just 2 divisions. Instead of the 440,000 Soviet soldiers in the G.D.R. we would have to deal with a more manageable complement of 220,000. The Soviet Union would then be presented with the possibility of doing something itself toward relaxing the quasi-truce between the two main victors of World War II. This process should lead to the complete withdrawal of Soviet forces behind their own borders by the turn of the century at the latest.

Following this, American troops could, in my view, be brought back home. One could imagine that in the course of the next few decades Western and Eastern Europe alike could be organized along the lines of stationary defense with sharply reduced tank components. No nation could invade the other. From the Soviet standpoint it would amount to a kind of reverse Finlandization of Eastern Europe. This could open up enormous room for political restructuring without it necessarily being immediately understood as a threat to the status quo.

By the turn of the century, at least, the conventional defense of Western Europe should be in the hands of the West Europeans. A certain reliance on the U.S. nuclear umbrella, possibly also a limited physical presence of conventional U.S. troops, for example, in geotactically precarious Berlin, might still be necessary. The East European communist regimes should by then be able to stand on their feet. Their own security system should likewise no longer be dependent on the Soviet Union. They would have to be able to cope with the domestic political turbulence in their own houses on their own. Of course, the West then must not seek to exploit any point of weakness in the Eastern systems, including in the intra-German relationship, and should not be able to exploit any such weaknesses militarily. From this perspective a change in Western defense structures toward a "structural non-aggression capability" is logically indicated. Anyone bent on destabilizing, and possibly exploiting destabilization militarily sometime in the future, will be providing for the perpetuation of Europe's division into two heavily armed, antagonistic social orders in the firm grip of at least one, if not both, of the two superpowers. It must be in our interest as Europeans, both East and West, to eliminate this state of affairs by concerted step-by-step efforts in the years to come.

The editor would like to thank Dennis Mercer for his professional translation of this essay.

General Sir Hugh Beach
On Improving NATO Strategy

In any discussion of the defense of Western Europe, the first question that must be addressed is: What is the source and nature of the threat? A simple answer would be that the preponderant conventional military strength of the Soviet Union poses the threat to Western Europe. But such a response overlooks some fundamental questions. These are not questions on which opinions in Europe and the United States are necessarily at variance, but since they are basic to any discussion of European defense, it will be useful to get them out of the way first.

Soviet intentions toward Western Europe are governed, it seems, less by any master plan than by a number of simple and deeply held convictions. The experience of successive invasions, which since the Mongol-Tartar domination have never succeeded, but which have led in recent centuries to ever-mounting tallies of death and destruction, has led the Soviet leadership to place its faith in massive military power—particularly on land—and in overinsurance on defense. As in most imperial systems at the point of their greatest expansion, there is a temptation to push frontiers outward, to create buffer zones, and to secure, as far as possible, the existence of compliant regimes in neighboring nations.

The Soviets ended World War II with a ready-made defensive glacis in Eastern Europe that provided a source of manpower, raw materials, and an industrial infrastructure that no subsequent Soviet government could contemplate relinquishing. The principal aims of policy have therefore been to consolidate Soviet suzerainty in Eastern Europe and to formalize the division of Germany—and both aims have been largely underwritten by the Helsinki accords. When the Soviets probed beyond these limits—as in their crude postwar attempt to drive the Western allies from Berlin—they found themselves confronted by a military defensive alliance system without precedent in peacetime. Constructed under the Brussels Treaty of 1948 and the North Atlantic Treaty of 1949, this alliance system is still in existence today.

Since the immediate postwar period there has been no evidence whatsoever that the Soviets have planned to extend their territories westward by force of arms. Nevertheless it is quite clear to them, for the simplest of geopolitical reasons, that the western peninsulas and islands of the Eurasian continent belong rightfully within their sphere of influence. The Americans have their own continent to look after. Accordingly, the Soviets believe they have a *right* to oversee what happens in Western Europe and to influence matters in their interest. Moreover, they believe that history is on their side, having discovered in Marxism-Leninism the scientific rules that govern it. Hence they are in no hurry—though they are not beyond giving history a helping hand where the correlation of forces seems propitious; no doubt on the principle that dialectical materialism helps those who help themselves.

Thus the arenas in which this East-West contest is to be played out are economic, social and political. As it happens these aspects of the Soviet system hold little power over the West, either to attract or threaten. On the economic front, the U.S.S.R. controls no unique source of raw materials nor channel of commerce. There are important links of East-West trade, of which the gas pipeline is a conspicuous example, but none constituting a major lever of economic influence or blackmail. On the social front, Western Europe finds the Soviet system profoundly antipathetic—for all its apparent emphasis on full employment, justice, brotherhood and human rights. All the evidence shows that the Soviet system fears, almost above all else, the infection of its own people with the social values of the West. Why else does Moscow continue to jam radio broadcasts, restrict telephone calls, minimize supplies of Western newspapers and magazines, and even control, as best it can, social contacts between Western visitors and Soviet citizens? And in the struggle for political influence in the West the track record of Marxism-Leninism has been uniformly poor. For many decades the Communist Party of Great Britain has failed to secure the election of a single candidate to Parliament. Nor are the so-called Eurocommunist parties of France or Italy within striking distance of taking power other than as minor partners in a coalition.

It follows that insofar as the U.S.S.R. excels in any sphere to the point where it poses a threat to the West, it is precisely not in the economic, social or political realms per se. Rather the threat the U.S.S.R. poses lies in *realpolitik*—i.e., the purchase to be gained by conventional military strength. It further follows that the best strategy available to the West consists in maintaining its own cohesion, self-confidence and self-respect; trusting in its own strength in the socio-economic fields in order to win the political contest in the long run; but meanwhile being wary of conceding to the Soviet Union any military option to which the Atlantic Alliance has literally no effective counter.

I. The Military Balance

It is beyond the scope of this book to discuss the question of the central strategic nuclear balance. Suffice it to say that now a situation of approximate balance, symmetry, equivalence or parity exists and is likely to continue into the foreseeable future. It is also true that the West has sufficient military force to cope with any border incident, even if mounted in strength and out of the blue at the beginning of a long weekend. So at both ends of the spectrum of violence the West can enjoy a high degree of confidence, and it offers the Warsaw Pact no easy ride. The worst case for NATO planning—i.e., the situation in which the Soviets come closest to having a military option that the West could not readily counter—would be a massive Warsaw Pact rolling advance across the frontiers of West Germany, directed upon the Ruhr industrial area and ultimately the Channel ports. It is not suggested that such an attack is plausible, let alone likely: indeed for reasons given earlier most people would rate any such contingency (so long as NATO holds together and keeps up its guard) as very improbable indeed. The point is, rather, that any such episode would be so catastrophic to the whole Western system as to provide the obligatory test case against which all force planning must be evaluated. This essay accordingly concentrates on the problems of the Central Front, not because the flanks are unimportant but because the center is normative.

The military equation can now be brought into sharper focus. Because of its obsession with massive military strength and overinsurance, its need to secure the compliance of the satellite regimes in Eastern Europe, and in the hope of exercising influence over Western Europe, the Soviet Union maintains a huge establishment of conventional military forces facing West. General Leopold Chalupa, the West German Commander-in-Chief of Allied Forces Central Europe, has recently assessed the resulting imbalance in conventional forces as follows, "Considering all our reinforcements and even the commitment of French forces, the ratio of land forces would quickly increase from about 2:1 to over 3:1 in favor of the Warsaw Pact, and for air forces he [sic] would enjoy an advantage of about 2.5 to 1 from the outset."[1]

We encounter at this point a peculiar paradox. On the one hand, common sense would suggest that for the purposes of a strategic assault by the Warsaw Pact upon Western Europe, a favorable force ratio of between two and three to one is no guarantee whatever of quick and easy success. This is a judgment never concurred in by the military authorities of NATO. The military view has always been that, given a fairly substantial Warsaw Pact incursion, properly orchestrated and in accordance with Soviet doctrine (though without use of nuclear weapons by either side), Western defenses would become incoherent within a matter of days rather than weeks, and Western reserves exhausted well before the Warsaw Pact ran out of steam. Which viewpoint is the better founded? Proponents of both points of view agree that NATO, as the putative defender, must cover the whole front of some 600 kilometers in Central Europe, whereas

---

[1]"The Defence of Central Europe: Implications of Change," lecture given at the Royal United Service for Defence Studies (RUSI), November 13, 1984. Reprinted in *RUSI*, March 1984, p. 14.

the Soviets, as attackers, could concentrate upon relatively few thrust lines—as in the German blitzkrieg—and thus build up overwhelming numerical superiority at decisive points. It is also clear that because of the Atlantic Ocean, NATO cannot trade space for time in the sense of adopting the strategy—ultimately used by the Soviets so successfully against the blitzkrieg—of defense in great depth.

The abandonment of large tracts of territory, even were there a good chance of eventual reconquest, is a most unappealing prospect. Consequently a policy of "forward defense" for NATO is politically indispensable. At the very least NATO must deny to the Warsaw Pact the prospect of any quick, easy gains or faits accomplis.

There is room for legitimate disagreement in assessing the balance of conventional forces (or "correlation of forces" in Soviet terminology) in three main areas. The first is in the value to be accorded to the non-Soviet, Warsaw Pact forces in Eastern Europe. No one can be sure whether, come the day, these forces will be loyal allies of the Soviet Union (which is clearly the worst-case assumption for NATO), or effectively neutral, or in overt opposition. It is, in any case, particularly difficult to generalize about a group of such disparate nations.

The second ground for disagreement concerns the extent to which the Warsaw Pact, by the outbreak of war, would have mobilized (possibly under the guise of large-scale maneuvers); the extent to which, if at all, the NATO allies would have done the same; and the degree of tactical surprise obtained in the assault. The difference in numerical force levels between the most optimistic and the most pessimistic readings of these two parameters is of huge significance.

Over and above this, there are a number of more technical factors relating to the detailed comparison of forces on the two sides such as the ratios of "teeth" to "tail"; relative states of training and tactical doctrine; the effectiveness of artillery, anti-tank weapons, ground-attack aircraft and helicopters against enemy armor; the adequacy of logistic provision; the sortie rate, kill rate and survivability of ground-attack aircraft; the Soviet preponderance in chemical munitions; the weight to be placed upon morale—when one side is defending its homeland while the other is the aggressor; the effectiveness of command, control, communications and intelligence (C^3I) functions in the headquarters of the two sides; and many others. Two things can be said with some confidence. First, the existence of these many imponderable and indeed unforeseeable factors in the equation is more than sufficient to account for the radical disagreements that we have noted concerning the likely outcome of any such encounter. Second, it is hard to fault military opinion in concluding that the duration of a successful and coherent defense *might* be measured in days rather than in weeks or months. As a worst-case analysis it is at least plausible.

Making all due allowance for Soviet objectives and misgivings and those of its allies, and making whatever reservations may be appropriate concerning technical military factors, the Warsaw Pact has the capacity to disrupt the integrity of NATO defenses by conventional assault within a week or so of starting. The political aim of military provision is to deny the Soviet Union, under any circumstances, the prospect of quick, easy gains or faits accomplis. To do this by means that carry a reasonable prospect of success, there is plainly a gap, or more accurately perhaps, an overhang, that needs to be offset.

In the early days of the Alliance, at Lisbon in 1952, the force goals adopted by NATO amounted to 96 Divisions—roughly the equivalent of the Soviet and East European forces confronting them from that time to this. If the military were given a free hand, it may well be that a similar bill would be presented today as the price of providing an all-conventional defense capable of defeating, beyond peradventure, any Warsaw Pact assault that did not include nuclear weapons.[2] There has never been the faintest likelihood that the NATO nations would provide anything approaching the Lisbon targets, and only two years later the figure was revised to 30 standing divisions in the central sector. Even that reduced total has never been met in peacetime and could be reached only slowly in wartime.

---

[2]In fairness to the planners, the Warsaw Pact enjoys a huge superiority in provision for offensive *chemical* warfare that could greatly hamper NATO's capacity for maneuver.

Meanwhile the overhang in question has been offset by the *deus ex machina* of battlefield or tactical nuclear weapons. The weapons themselves are real enough and have been provided—almost entirely by the United States—to fill a huge variety of ecological niches on the battlefield. There are nuclear warheads for shells, rockets, surface and anti-aircraft missiles, nuclear landmines, depth charges and free-falling aircraft bombs. For a number of years there have been surface-to-surface cruise missiles (Matador and Mace—currently Tomahawk) and during the early 1960s, there was even a nuclear mortar whimsically entitled Davy Crockett. Their numbers built up rather slowly, but by the 1970s the total of tactical nuclear warheads fielded by NATO—including some provided by Great Britain for its own aircraft—had risen to some 7,000.

At the same time, a matching doctrine was gradually developed. In 1954, and for a dozen years thereafter, NATO planning was officially based on the principle that nuclear weapons would be used tactically in reply to almost any aggression. This was, perhaps, rational so long as it was assumed that any war in Europe would automatically lead to global nuclear war: a strategy (if it can be so designated) of the "tripwire." By the mid-1960s, however, the Soviets acquired the ability to strike American territory with nuclear weapons, thus depriving the tripwire strategy of all credibility. Over a period of some ten years, culminating in December 1967, a new and more plausible strategy was slowly evolved. Known as "flexible response," it is still applied to this day. This doctrine relies upon conventional forces to counter any Soviet non-nuclear attack as far forward as possible and to allow time for reinforcements to arrive. The function of theater nuclear forces is to provide a link between the conventional and the strategic nuclear forces, providing options short of a strategic exchange and deterring use of theater nuclear forces by the other side.

Flexible Response

For all its intellectual incoherence the doctrine of flexible response has one major achievement to its credit. It would be too much to claim that it has kept the peace. This has been achieved by the political solidarity of the North Atlantic powers, the physical presence on the continent of some half a million American souls,[3] and the U.S. nuclear "guarantee." But what flexible response has done is to enable Europeans to keep their nerve at a far lower level of conventional force provision than might otherwise have been required. The money so saved has been spent on universities, motorways, hospitals, manufacturing investment or private consumption, according to taste—by any standard a highly desirable, not to say *moral*, redistribution of funds.

The problems of flexible response begin when one starts to evaluate it, not simply as an ingredient in the panoply of deterrence, but as a program for action were deterrence to fail. At least one of the original architects of flexible response, former Secretary of Defense Robert McNamara, wanted to place the onus for "escalation" (i.e., first-use of nuclear weapons) upon the aggressor. He failed to carry his point. So it remains the essence of flexible response that, if and when conventional defense were visibly failing and reserves approaching exhaustion, the political authorities of NATO would be expected to accede to the request for what is ghoulishly known as nuclear "release." In other words, if there were no other way of stopping the Warsaw Pact, NATO would be prepared to initiate nuclear war. What would then follow?

The simple and obvious answer is that nobody can possibly know. The current British White Paper on Defence, in dealing with this point, states that the object of escalation (if necessary) would be to convince the aggressor that he had miscalculated NATO's resolve and should "cease his attack and withdraw."[4] This concept implies that one or more nuclear weapons would be used to knock out enemy airfields, major bridges or reinforcing formations, possibly in Poland. This might so horrify the Soviet leadership, bringing home to them the perils to their own people and the determination of NATO to resist at all costs, that they would decide to back away and stop the war. Certainly this is a possible outcome: one which the Soviets are bound to take seriously in any calculus of peace and war. And a first-use of nu-

---

[3] Actually 325,000 U.S. Army and Air Force men and women and their dependents.

[4] *Statement on the Defence Estimates, 1985*, HMSO, Cmnd 9430–1, p. 12.

clear weapons that had this consequence would be both rational and moral: rational because it would achieve the required political objective; moral because it would bring the war to an end far more cheaply—in terms of human life—than could be done by any conventional means. On the other hand, as former West German Chancellor Helmut Schmidt pointed out in a book he wrote while the doctrine of flexible response was crystallizing, "Who could complain if the Soviet high command, in response to destructive attacks on the Vistula Bridges involving the (albeit unintentional) widespread devastation of Warsaw proceeded simultaneously to destroy the Elbe and Rhine crossings and in so doing produced similar devastation in Hamburg, Cologne, Dusseldorf? And if we wish to lodge a complaint to what tribunal shall we take it?"[5] To this question there has never been a satisfactory answer.

The Soviets have always said—as their tactical doctrine and training require—that any use of nuclear weapons by NATO would be met by at least an equivalent response on the part of the Warsaw Pact and possibly with interest. One aim, in so saying, is doubtless to counter NATO strategy. But as prudent planners they must have taken into consideration from the outset that NATO might employ some of its battlefield nuclear weapons. Unless they had hopelessly misjudged Alliance cohesion, they would only have gone to war in the first place if the alternative seemed even more dire. How can one be sure that their nerve would then crack first? If it did not, the likelihood of further escalation must be rated highly, not excluding eventual recourse to strategic nuclear weapons.

A first-use that had this consequence would be neither rational nor moral. It would stand every chance of destroying precisely that system of Western values that is the whole aim of the strategy to defend. Since it is by definition impossible to know in advance which, out of a whole spectrum of possible outcomes, would be most likely to result (one cannot exclude some outcomes that would involve the destruction of German civilization at the least), this very uncertainty—useful as it may be in the context of deterrence—imports a large element of the implausi-

---

[5]*Defence or Retaliation*, Edinburgh: Oliver & Boyd, 1962, p. 99.

ble and the irrational into the whole concept of deliberate escalation or first-use.

It is also irrational because, on the evidence of war games and operational analysis, if NATO used nuclear weapons and the Soviets did no more than retaliate like for like, the Soviets advance, though it might be held up temporarily, could fairly soon be resumed more effectively than before. The reason is simple. Nuclear war increases attrition, and attrition favors the "big battalions." It is implausible because the decision to "go nuclear" would require, at the very least, the concurrence of the heads of government of the United States and the principal states of Western Europe.[6] Securing Alliance unanimity upon such issues as the European gas pipeline, the Moscow Olympics, cruise missiles and the neutron bomb has proved hard enough. In this instance the very survival of peoples would be at stake. The decision to initiate would be the most difficult and divisive that any group of people would have been called upon to take. They would need time. Military men in NATO have therefore been tempted to assume that the idea of going nuclear, before the coherence of the defense had been irretrievably lost, is purest moonshine.

The doctrine is also ethically perverse. This is not because there is anything to choose, ethically, between first-use and retaliation as such. Everything hinges on the outcome, as has already been explained. There is, however, an element of perversity in seeking to deter nuclear war by the stated intention, however conditional, of invoking it. For these reasons there has always been pressure from men of clear sight and goodwill (following McNamara and Schmidt) to move NATO away from the concept of "deliberate escalation." The alternatives have been variously described: "raising the nuclear threshold," "no-early-use," or "no-first-use" are current variants.

All have in common the intention to de-emphasize the part to be played by nuclear weapons upon the battlefield. All seek to

---

[6]The suggestion that in these circumstances the president of the United States might elect unilaterally to go nuclear upon the European battlefield seems to this writer implausible and mischievous in the highest degree.

improve the effectiveness of conventional forces. But it is at this point that two crucial distinctions become necessary. The first applies to those proponents of no-first-use who advocate joining the Soviet Union, as they have repeatedly proposed, in a joint declaration to this effect. This was precisely the burden of the key resolution passed by the General Synod of the Church of England by a vote of 387 to 49 calling upon NATO "publicly to forswear" first-use of nuclear weapons in any circumstances.[7] A declaration of this kind would be precisely the wrong sort of arms control measure to pursue—declaratory, unverifiable, and not altering the price of fish by one kopeck. And in the unlikely event that it were to be taken seriously by the Soviets it would, to that extent, undermine deterrence.

Equally imprudent would be any measure purporting to eliminate nuclear weapons totally from the defensive concept of the West and to change to a non-nuclear strategy. Some means of bringing nuclear fire to bear upon the battlefield is needed, both to deter the Soviets from using their nuclear firepower first and as an economical means of imposing dispersion upon any Warsaw Pact incursions, which is clearly favorable to the defense. But this is not to say that battlefield nuclear weapons, in anything approaching their existing numbers and types, will continue to be necessary—or even required at all upon the European mainland. The F–111 or Tornado strike aircraft stationed in the United Kingdom; air, land, sea- or submarine-launched cruise missiles, or ballistic-missile-firing submarines could well suffice.

What is proposed here has been well described by Lawrence Freedman in a contribution to this series. "What does make sense is for NATO to plan its military operations on the presumption that nuclear forces *will not be used* and *should not be needed*" (emphasis added).[8] There have always been and will al-

---

[7]*The Church and the Bomb*, The General Synod Debate, February 1983, London: Church of England Information Office, 1983, p. 67.

[8]See "U.S. Nuclear Weapons in Europe: Symbols, Strategy and Force Structure," in Andrew J. Pierre, ed., *Nuclear Weapons in Europe*, New York: Council on Foreign Relations, Inc., 1984, p. 68.

ways be those who see more danger than virtue in this suggestion on the grounds that it could make war more acceptable and thus more likely. With the 40th anniversary of the ending of World War II fresh in everyone's mind this is an unappealing prospect—not least for the Germans. But this is not an objection that appears logical when compared to the careful and limited form of no-first-use proposed by Professor Freedman. The reason has been well expounded by General Bernard W. Rogers, Supreme Allied Commander Europe, who writes that "by establishing the credible prospect that an ACE [Allied Command Europe] conventional response might succeed, our deterrent posture will be enhanced and the nuclear threshold raised."[9] In other words the risk not only of a nuclear war but of any war will be lessened. This is a wholly rational objective. Whether it amounts to a revision of flexible response is an open question and only important in the context of presentation. Probably the wisest course is to regard it as an enhancement of flexible response, bringing it closer to its pristine form—at least as envisaged by McNamara. We turn now to the practicalities.

II. Enhancing Conventional Defense

The recent upsurge of discussion on providing a self-reliant conventional defense has focused upon three separate conceptual aspects albeit closely interwoven. These are proposals for *troop* enhancements, the contribution to be made by *"emerging technology"* and revised and improved *tactical* schemes. We consider these in turn.

Troop Enhancements

There is nothing novel in the suggestion that NATO should aim for higher force levels on the Central Front (indeed this harks back to Lisbon in 1952) nor in the idea, which is not quite the

---

[9]"Follow-On Forces Attack (FOFA): Myths and Realities," *NATO Review*, December 1984, p. 9.

same thing, that the Europeans should at least contribute more. It has been an abiding strand in American thinking that willingness to commit a large hostage presence in Europe, coupled with the nuclear guarantee implicit in the terms of the Atlantic Treaty itself,[10] is predicated upon the Europeans themselves contributing enough to ensure a robust conventional defense of their own territory. If it were not so, then America could get caught up in a spiral of escalation, placing her own people at dire risk.

Meanwhile, as the countries of Western Europe have become progressively more prosperous there has been much sympathy in Congress for the proposition that the Europeans can afford to do more to help themselves. While this is a strong perception, nourished perhaps by the latent isolationism not too deeply buried in the American psyche, it is not altogether fair. In fact according to British government estimates, the European members of NATO contribute toward the ready forces stationed in Europe 90 percent of the manpower, 85 percent of the tanks, 95 percent of the artillery and 80 percent of the combat aircraft—not to mention 85 percent of all warships in the Atlantic and European waters.[11] But fair or no, much of the American pressure in recent decades upon its European allies to do more in the field of conventional defenses has taken the petulant—not to say perverse—form of threatening to take some U.S. forces away.

From 1966 to 1973 Senator Mike Mansfield persisted with a resolution calling for a reduction of U.S. forces in Europe, and in 1973 it almost carried—but the onset of negotiations with the Soviet Union on Mutual and Balanced Force Reductions (MBFR) defused this issue for a time. The Carter Administration took a far more constructive line and at the NATO summit in 1977 secured agreement on a major initiative—the Long-Term Defense Program. This called for coordinated actions to improve conventional forces across almost the whole spectrum—specifically, and in the jargon, these included readiness, reinforcement, reserves, mobilization, maritime posture, air defense, C^3I, elec-

---

[10]Essentially this provides that "an armed attack against one or more of [the parties] in Europe ... shall be considered an attack against them all."

[11]*Statement on the Defence Estimates, 1985, op. cit.*, p. 15.

tronic warfare, logistics and rationalization. Even more to the point, perhaps, member-nations undertook to increase their defense expenditures, *in real terms,* by an annual amount "in the region of three per cent," and these commitments have been reendorsed every two years thereafter.[12]

All this was not without its ironies. The intention was to spur the European allies to do better. Yet during the 1970s the Europeans had been improving their defense inputs by an average of around three percent annually, so the figure was selected for that reason. It was the American defense contribution that had been on a post-Vietnam decline. Nevertheless, whatever its rationale, the Long-Term Defense Program was a wholly constructive measure from which much benefit has come.

More recently, congressional efforts to impel the European members of NATO to do more in their own defense have reverted to a more backhanded method. In June 1984 Senator Sam Nunn, himself a staunch supporter of the Alliance, introduced an amendment mandating an annual reduction of 30,000 American troops in Europe in each of the years 1987, 1988 and 1989, *unless* the European allies continued to meet the three percent annual real growth rate in defense spending. As an alternative, in the event that the three percent target was not met, the withdrawals could be waived if the U. S. Secretary of Defense was able to certify that certain, carefully specified, steps had been taken to improve ammunition stockpiles, to increase the number of aircraft shelters provided by host nations for American reinforcing aircraft, and most interestingly, "to improve conventional defense capacity which contributes to lengthening the time period between an armed attack on any NATO country and the time the Supreme Allied Commander would have to request the release and use of nuclear weapons."[13] This last is a succinct portrayal of the theme of this chapter. The amendment did not carry, but it did attract 4l votes, and without strenuous lobbying by the Reagan Administration, would have done still better. It

---

[12]Ministerial Guidance, May 18, 1977. Most recently in M–DPC–1(85)10 of May 22, 1985.

[13]*Congressional Record,* June 20, 1984, p. S7721.

represents a line of thinking that will not go away.

Against this background it is easy to dispose of that class of proposal that looks simply to the provision of more tanks, guns and tactical aircraft as a means of offsetting the conventional imbalance. Over the years there has been no shortage of such suggestions. One of the more interesting was that propounded by *The Economist* in 1982.[14] On the strength, it said, of a wide-ranging canvas of military opinion in various countries, *The Economist* came up with a shopping list of additional matériel needed "to fight a solid defensive battle on the central front for 30 days." The answer came out that the extra weapons and the men needed to fight with them could be acquired at a cost of a further 1 to 1.5 percent annual real growth on top of the 3 percent already pledged.

Other proposals for enhanced force levels have come from the fertile pens of William Kaufmann[15] and the indefatigable analyst Steven Canby.[16] All these ignore two simple facts. The first is that any net increases in force levels, to the extent that they were real and not cosmetic, would fly in the face of all that has been attempted in ten years of discussion on MBFR at Vienna and, to the extent that the U.S.S.R. took them seriously, would most likely lead to the Soviets raising the ante to match. This would simply result in a greater expense on both sides without achieving greater security and would be utterly self-defeating.

Equally relevant is the fact that the three percent pledge itself has proved to be overambitious. In 1979 the average increase for all NATO nations other than the United States was 2.2 percent. In 1980 and 1981 it was 2.7 percent.[17] In 1982 and 1983 it was between 1 percent and 1.6 percent. In the United Kingdom the de-

---

[14]"Do you seriously want to be non-nuclear?" *The Economist,* July 31, 1982.

[15]See "Nonnuclear Deterrence" in John D. Steinbruner and Leon V. Sigal, eds., *Alliance Security: NATO and the No-First-Use Question,* Washington, D.C.: The Brookings Institution, 1983, pp. 43–91.

[16]"Military Reform and the Art of War," *Survival,* May/June 1983, p. 122.

[17]*Allied Contributions to The Common Defense,* March 1983, Report to U.S. Congress by Caspar W. Weinberger, Secretary of Defense, Washington, D.C., 1983, pp. 50–51.

fense budget will have grown, between 1978–1979 and 1985–1986, by roughly three percent a year in real terms (including the Falkland Islands War expenditure) but the commitment ceases at that point.[18]

The British Chief of Defense Staff, Field Marshal Sir Edwin Bramall, has explained that in his opinion this leveling off will result in a future decline in the amount of defense capability purchased.[19] The primary reasons for this are that new technology is always more expensive than that which it replaces, so the unit replacement cost of prime equipment rises in real terms.[20] Likewise the cost of manpower rises in real terms, in line with the standard of living generally. In the United Kingdom, as in all the NATO countries involved in the Central Front, the size of the age group from which the armed services are recruited will fall dramatically in the next ten years. The high standards necessarily demanded in an all-volunteer army mean that even with high unemployment there will be no surplus of readily recruitable young people over the next decade. Subsidiary reasons include the deliberate squeeze on cash limits by an assumed rate of inflation (by the Treasury) lower than the actual one; the possibility of decline of the pound against the dollar; the sudden imposition of Value Added Tax on military construction work and services; certain costs at U.S. airfields; possibly a contribution toward the cost of British involvement in European space activities; and the effects of the program to purchase Trident. The effects, Sir Edwin said, might be a decline of as much as seven percent in volume terms from the current three percent growth. This is almost embarrassingly frank, and while there is plainly scope for flexibility in matching resources to programs from year to year, it is hard to believe that the implications can be fully absorbed.

It is not surprising that, in the Field Marshal's view, the nucle-

---

[18] *Statement on the Defence Estimates 1985, op. cit.*, pp. 33, 35.

[19] *House of Commons Defence Committee Hearings*, February 6, 1985, London, Paper 37–11, pp. 204–207.

[20] Between 6% and 10% a year according to *Statement on the Defence Estimates 1982*, vol. 1, Cmnd 8529–1, p. 27.

168 / The Conventional Defense of Europe

ar threshold would probably remain at roughly the same level, and that he sees General Rogers' statements as largely a case of reassuring the public. But all this, sensible and realistic as it undoubtedly is, presents the Alliance with an acute dilemma. On the one hand, there is the undoubted need, argued earlier in this essay, for a stronger conventional component, not least but not only, for the sake of public reassurance. On the other hand, we foresee the prospect—with one major European ally at least—of declining real outputs in the defense field despite the welcome efforts of the present U.S. Administration to increase the value for money obtained. If it is hard to fault Senator Nunn's objectives, it is equally clear that to persist in the bargaining approach of his amendment is likely to have precisely the reverse effect to what he wants. The dangers in the situation are plain and the prescription far from obvious. Indeed there *is* no solution along the lines of "more of the same," and it is under this goad that fresh hopes have come to be placed in the contributions that emerging technology might make.

Emerging Technology

The particular package that has been assembled under this generic title had its origins in the Reagan Administration's need to provide a new rejuvenating initiative to match Carter's Long-Term Defense Plan and the three percent pledge. It was put together by officials, in time for the December 1982 NATO ministerial meeting and was complemented soon afterward by an influential and independent group known as the European Security Study (ESECS).[21]

These make a persuasive technical case that a combination of improved and more discriminate shaped charge warheads applied to the submunitions dispersed by cluster weapons and allied with an autonomous homing capability, together with long-range target acquisition, pinpoint navigation, survivable

---

[21] *Strengthening Conventional Deterrence in Europe: Proposals for the 1980s,* Report of the European Security Study (ESECS), New York: St. Martin's, 1983.

communications, and computerized command and control, would make it possible to engage various target arrays by non-nuclear means that hitherto have only been possible to attack economically with nuclear warheads. These munitions would have few, if any, of the collateral effects of nuclear weapons such as blast, heat, neutron flux, and fallout. Hence they need not be subject to formal release procedures and would be employable from the outset of any hostilities. A further bonus could accrue from configuring these munitions so that they are delivered by shell, rocket, standoff bomb, or missile rather than by overflying aircraft, thus conserving NATO's most valuable resource (trained manpower) and uncoupling the delivery means from vast, conspicuous and vulnerable concrete runways with all the temptation to preemptive attack that these afford.

The emerging technology package has something in common with President Reagan's Strategic Defense Initiative (SDI). It looks far into the future, and it aims to substitute a conventional option for the balance of nuclear terror. The problems are also of a similar character: Can it be afforded? Will it work? What will happen when the Soviets take the same road? Can they circumvent it more cheaply? What are the implications for technology transfer, arms control, crisis management, and ultimately the stability of the international system?

At first presentation, and not surprisingly in view of the way it was put together, the Emerging Technology Initiative (ET) bore all the hallmarks of the American predilection for a technological "quick fix" with an underpinning of clear commercial advantage for the United States vis-à-vis Europe. There was great confusion over likely costs. U.S. Secretary of Defense Caspar Weinberger was reported as suggesting that ET could be exploited within existing resource guidelines. The ESECS follow-up report placed a $30 billion price-tag on its proposals to be spread over about ten years and shared among the member states.[22] General Rogers, in the same context, has argued that a four percent an-

---

[22]*Strengthening Conventional Deterrence in Europe: A Program for the 1980s*, European Security Study, Report of the Special Panel (ESECS II), Boulder, Colo.: Westview, 1985.

nual real increase in defense budgets throughout the 1980s could enable NATO to meet his criterion for high confidence in its ability to contain even a major Warsaw Pact attack,[23] but he appears since then to have amended this estimate to seven percent.

The plain fact is that, as with SDI and any other complex, innovative and disparate package of techniques, no one can tell in advance how much it will cost or exactly when it will be ready. The battlefield nuclear option does not come cheap for hardware. ET may well be cheaper. If so, it might indeed contribute both to raising the nuclear threshold and to alleviating the financial dilemma. In any case it would ill become the European partners to complain that the high technology in ET was all exploited to American advantage, leaving only the simpler items (rocket motors, airframes) to be made by the Europeans. There is no need for this whatever, and the remedy lies in European hands. Since 1979, under a package deal with the United States, three European firms[24] have been collaborating on an advanced anti-tank missile; since 1984 three European and one American firm have been engaged in development of terminally guided submunitions (a typical ET concept) for the latest Multiple Launch Rocket System.[25]

Consortia make for difficult working and some increase in expense—but the result is reduced development costs, longer production runs, greater standardization and interoperability, and an increase in the political cohesion of the Alliance. Moreover consortia that include an American industrial partner provide a useful means of outflanking the problem of technology transfer from the American to European firms. There is no doubt that this is the right way to go.

More substantial doubts concern the Soviet reaction to all this, under two headings. The first question is, will they develop similar systems themselves? Of this there seems little doubt.

---

[23]"The Atlantic Alliance: Prescriptions For A Difficult Decade," *Foreign Affairs*, Summer 1982.

[24]British Aerospace, Aerospatiale and Messerschmidt Bolkow Blohm.

[25]Thorn-EMI with the Royal Ordinance Factories, Thomson-Brandt, Diehl and Martin Marietta.

They always have. And former Chief-of-Staff of the Soviet armed forces, Marshal Nikolai A. Ogarkov's widely quoted interview with *Red Star* explicitly claimed, for the Soviet version of ET, almost precisely the same enhancement of conventional capabilities as General Rogers has advocated for the West.[26] Nor need this cause undue alarm. Indeed it does much to undermine the instant Soviet reaction that ET is dangerous, provocative, escalatory, blurs the threshold between conventional and nuclear war, and increases attrition. From their point of view there is some truth in all these contentions.

No doubt the Soviets would prefer that they could freely develop emerging technologies at their own pace, and that NATO did not. They would also prefer that a high nuclear threshold be maintained, thereby giving more political leverage to their conventional preponderance. But these objectives are incompatible. And whatever the Soviets decide, the main advantage to NATO will remain: namely, substituting the conventional for the nuclear in major strike systems and substituting missiles for manned aircraft.

Soviet countermeasures are a different matter. If it were to prove possible to defeat, for example, sensor systems in the far infrared or millimeter radar seekers—say by means of camouflage, spoofing, electronic countermeasures or opaque smoke (chaff)—or to neutralize surveillance, target acquisition, command, control or information systems by means that are much cheaper than the emerging technology systems themselves, then these systems would indeed have been a most expensive waste of money. But of this there is no clear evidence at the moment, and the problems are no different from those at the early stage of any new technology. It is up to the West to keep its nerve and to trust that, at least in these particular areas, which are mostly based upon microelectronics and highly sophisticated software, the West will maintain its technical edge in the foreseeable future.[27]

---

[26] *Red Star*, Moscow, May 9, 1984.

[27] It must be acknowledged that difficulties besetting the British Nimrod airborne early warning system are not a happy augury. But this experience is atypical.

A related problem concerns the implications of emerging technologies for crisis stability and arms control. If it is the intention to supply conventional warheads for weapons systems such as Lance and Tomahawk, which also carry nuclear warheads, how are these to be counted for arms control purposes? And come the day, how are the Russians to be persuaded that the missiles flying their way are in fact conventional? These are difficult problems, but probably not insoluble. A similar difficulty was encountered in identifying bombers equipped with air-launched cruise missiles and was solved by fitting them with identifiable airframe modifications. In the case of missiles a simple solution would be to permit inspection by observer teams. This would probably be acceptable to the West but very difficult for the Soviet Union.

If it is not possible to make conventional missiles visually or electronically distinctive, they could still be based quite separately from nuclear missiles with their conspicuous special storage sites.[28] Another possibility would be to undertake that all missiles of a range shorter than, say, 150 km would be conventional; over that range, nuclear. Or it might be agreed that all cruise missiles would be conventional, all ballistic missiles, nuclear. None of these suggestions is without problems, but neither is there reason to suppose, a priori, that solutions cannot be found.

The final question concerns the stability of the international system—but here we are back into the archetypal realm. Field Marshal Bramall (with General Chalupa) believes that, in terms of deterrence, a low nuclear threshold may be no bad thing since the aim is to prevent war, not to fight one.[29] Complacency on this score would be misplaced. NATO ministers, at the December 1984 meeting, called for a coherent effort to further improve conventional defenses. In addition, NATO military authorities are developing a "conceptual military framework" to better enable the setting of priorities for conventional defense improvements, including the sensible application of emerging

---

[28]*Strengthening Conventional Deterrence in Europe*, ESECS II, *op. cit.*, p. 123.

[29]*House of Commons Defence Committee Hearings, op. cit.*, p. 213.

technology.[30] This is encouraging and leads naturally to a consideration of tactical doctrine and concepts to match the developments that have been discussed above.

Tactical Doctrine

From one point of view there has been a high degree of coherence in the recent evolution of technical and tactical concepts in NATO. General Rogers has explained that as early as 1979 the staff at his headquarters began to develop a "sub-concept" for reducing—with conventional weapons—the number of enemy forces arriving in the forward area.[31]

Fresh impetus was given to this line of thought by the disclosure—notably in the Warsaw Pact exercise "Zapad 8l"—of a return by the Soviets to their World War II concept of "operational maneuver groups" as part of offensive doctrine. These groups, designed to be self-sustaining for a time, are used to penetrate weak points in the defense and then to operate against crucial elements such as headquarters and command posts, nuclear weapons delivery means, and logistic complexes. It is central to Soviet doctrine that fresh formations are continuously fed in to sustain the momentum of the offensive in the hope of cracking the defense apart before it can resort to nuclear weapons. Against this it is wholly logical to develop a concept for the early attack of reinforcing formations before they can reach the battlefield. This is precisely the aim of the sub-concept in question, now known as "Follow-on Forces Attack" (FOFA) and formally endorsed by the NATO Defense Planning Committee on November 9, 1984.

The immediate question to ask is what is new about this sub-concept? Interdiction of the enemy's rear area by way of attacks upon bridges and communication centers, airfields, and reinforcing formations have for many decades been part of military plans and doctrine. The means of attack has been manned aircraft. But air-defense radar and missiles are now so effective that deep penetration of enemy airspace is a very hazardous undertaking from which a high loss rate can be expected. NATO has

---

[30]*Statement on the Defence Estimates, 1985, op. cit.*, p. 10; and *The Times* (London), May 22, 1985, p. 9.

[31]"Follow-On Forces Attack (FOFA): Myths and Realities", *op. cit.* pp. 1–9.

too few aircraft capable of these missions and a high loss rate cannot be sustained.

It is no accident, therefore, that in military terms the case for early-first-use of nuclear weapons has been precisely in this deep strike mode. And it is precisely in this mode that emerging technology concepts have the most obvious attraction. Non-nuclear weapons systems are under development that have specific and various capabilities. They can attack airfield runways, aircraft shelters, aircraft and repair machinery; communication centers and radar sites; bridges, railways lines, marshalling yards, and matériel dumps; and reinforcing formations, even when they are on the move—all to a depth of 100 or 200 kilometers behind enemy lines. And all these specialized munitions can be married up with any known type of delivery system such as shells, rockets, surface-to-surface missiles, and cruise or ballistic missiles.

Clearly a strong conceptual framework is needed to govern these developments in which the common theme is that the warheads are non-nuclear and the delivery means unmanned. It is precisely to provide a framework of this kind that the FOFA doctrine has been devised. Even so, a number of very difficult questions remain. There is the question of the balance of investment. How much technical effort and finance is it right to commit to deep strike in comparison with the upgrading of defenses against the enemy front line of attack—where urgency is arguably even more pressing? Senator Nunn's emphasis on ammunition stockpiles and aircraft shelters as prime contributions to raising the nuclear threshold was certainly not misplaced. How realistic is it to suppose that political approval will be forthcoming automatically, or at any early stage, for the release of flocks of missiles, albeit non-nuclear, bound several hundred kilometers into Warsaw Pact territory? And how feasible an operation of war is the attack of *mobile* forces deep in enemy territory?

The concepts so far explored involve a degree of complexity in the linking of reconnaissance aircraft, radar, command posts, computers, missile sites, and the missiles themselves in flight, which seems to many skeptics—this writer included—excessive to the point of unreality. All this will no doubt come out in the wash—and all the more quickly insofar as the European countries involve themselves not only in the conceptual discussions but in the research and development activity itself. It is encouraging that political agreement was reached in May 1984 to proceed with 11 projects under the ET Initiative in the fields of surveillance and communications as well as precision artillery. To this extent, at least, technical and doctrinal developments are indeed in a fair degree of congruence.

The note of discord is struck by the existence in the United States of what appears to be a quite different doctrine, referred to in the shorthand as "Airland Battle."[32] Originating in the U.S. Army's Training and Doctrine Command, this concept purports to describe how U.S. corps and divisions would fight the battle in meeting the *worldwide* commitments of the United States. Ostensibly this doctrine was developed under the guidance of General Donn A. Starry to replace the preexisting doctrine known as "active defense," which had come to be seen as dangerously linear, static and reactive. By contrast Airland Battle emphasizes maneuver, agility and decentralized control. It recognizes that some enemy breakthroughs are inevitable. It underscores the value of counterattack deep in enemy territory. Most controversially, it stresses the importance of integrating nuclear with non-nuclear means. "By extending the battlefield, and integrating conventional, nuclear, chemical and electronic means ... the U.S. Army can *quickly* begin offensive action to conclude the battle on its terms."[33] It can then be represented as a doctrine directly aimed at lowering the nuclear threshold.

General Rogers has seen this danger. In a forthright article he has set out to explain that all forces that would come under his command in war would operate under his doctrine, policy and concepts, which differ from Airland Battle in three crucial respects:

—We do not plan for the integrated use of conventional, nuclear and chemical weapons in ACE. We make a clear distinction be-

---

[32] *Field Manual FM 100–5: Operations,* U.S. Army Training and Doctrine Command (TRADOC), Washington, D.C., August 1982; and *U.S. Army Concepts for the Airland Battle and Corps '86,* TRADOC, Para 525-5, March 25, 1981.

[33] *Field Manual FM 100–5, op. cit.* pp. 1–5.

tween conventional and mass destruction weapons. Any use by the Alliance of either chemical or nuclear weapons would always be in accordance with release procedures approved by Alliance political authorities.

—We will not engage in preemptive strikes. NATO is a defensive alliance and as such will never fire the first shot. Contrary to popular perception we will not attack across our borders with ground forces heading deep into the enemy's rear area.

—We will, however, use the counterattack—the essence of a viable defence—to restore our borders.[34]

This is both clearly and, in some respects, bravely said. But it is really not good enough. What is needed is a statement, by U.S. military and political authorities, explicitly disavowing these aspects of Airland Battle in the European context.[35] It is a lame and quite insufficient excuse to plead that Airland Battle is a low-level operational concept for use worldwide.

There is, however, a totally different conceptual framework in which at least, some, of the fruits of emerging technology could be applied. This also has its roots in the early years of the Alliance. In 1954 a plan was floated by Colonel Bogislav von Bonin whereby the West German Army would have consisted of an all-volunteer force, about 150,000 strong, equipped with anti-tank weapons and formed into defensive units, *Sperrverbande*, for deployment as a continuous screen within 50 kilometers of the zonal border. They were to constitute a covering force behind which mobile allied forces could mount their counterattack.[36] The linear characteristic of the proposed screen was an obvious weakness, but the idea of a semi-static matrix of local defense was picked up and given more precision by Sir Basil Liddell Hart in the early 1960s.[37] He envisaged

---

[34] "Follow-On Forces Attack (FOFA): Myths and Realities", *op. cit.*, p. 7.

[35] *Improving NATO's Conventional Capabilities*, Report to the Congress, U.S. Department of Defense, June 1984, mentions only the restriction of maneuver space and concentration of air effort—quite different points.

[36] Hans Spier, *German Re-Armament and Atomic War*, Evanston, Illinois: Row Peterson & Co., 1957, pp. 75–77.

[37] *Deterrent or Defence*, London: Stevens & Son, 1960, pp. 165–173.

a deep network of defense posts in the forward zone being manned—if necessary, at short notice—by a citizen militia of the Swiss type. This, he thought, he would allow a useful reduction in the number of main shield force divisions to be fielded by the remainder of the Alliance. The concept of guerrilla and mechanized forces, under a single operational command and working to a common plan was worked up further ten years later by then-Colonel E.A. Burgess—now General Sir Edward Burgess, deputy to General Rogers.[38]

His scheme was one of the earliest to give due credit to a notable feature of large parts of central Germany—its unique suitability for defensive use. The German landscape includes large tracts of difficult country: the Harz Mountains, Grosses Moor (peat bog), Hoch Sauerland, the Franconian Jura and many areas of timber-covered ridges that surround the North German plain. There are huge areas of suburban sprawl, increasing daily. There are many hundreds of square miles of agricultural land with settlements in villages a few kilometers apart on a quasi-geometrical pattern. All these are ideal for defense by small sub-units, with local knowledge, using the techniques that the German Army displayed with such brilliance (for example, in the Normandy bocage and east of Caen) in the summer of 1944. In his scheme the main onus for providing the territorial defense network would fall upon the Federal Republic—no doubt with some compensating reduction in that country's contribution to forces provided for the mobile armed battle.

More recently the point has been made that modern technology could assist this concept in at least two ways. The first would be by "landscaping" to create obstacles specifically designed to prevent a rapid breakthrough by tanks. These preparations could include the laying of pipe drains to be filled in an emergency by liquid explosives to blow instant anti-tank ditches; the preparation of small earth emplacements of the kind so well used by the Israelis against the Syrians on the Golan; even tree-planting, albeit this is a somewhat longer term measure. All this pays due deference to political objections in the Federal Republic to any preparations seeming to symbolize the per-

---

[38]Brigadier D.M. Pontifex and Colonel E.A. Burgess, *British Army Review*, no. 35, August 1970.

178 / The Conventional Defense of Europe

petual division of Germany. If this somewhat naïve objection were withdrawn, then much more could be done (without ecological penalty) by way of permanent obstacles, emplacements and observation posts. This would in no way be a case of yielding to Maginot-line mentality. On the contrary, it would be a prudent, relatively cheap, and unambiguously defensive (and thus wholly non-provocative) way of economizing in terms of lives, maintaining the nuclear threshold, and deterring war.

The second way in which modern technology could contribute to a militia-guerrilla network concept of static defense as a complement to existing mobile concepts would be by opening up possibilities for highly effective, small, shoulder-fired anti-tank and anti-aircraft missiles; for more secure communications; and for rapidly and remotely emplaced anti-tank and anti-personnel mines. Modern technology can also provide a means of detecting enemy movement by small unmanned sensor systems as well as a means of rapid support and reinforcement through helicopter gunships and heli-borne forces. It is therefore not surprising that the 1980s has seen a fresh crop of proposals, all of which, in essence, capitalize on the idea of a network of lightly armed forces, using a mix of conventional and quasi-guerrilla tactics in concert with troops designed for the more familiar mobile armored operations. Afheldt, Spannocchi, Brossollet and Löser have all contributed.[39] Most recently Franz Uhle-Wettler, now Commander of the Panzer Division, in his book *Gefechtsfeld Mitteleuropa (Battlefield Central Europe)* has put forward a variant of this concept, which has been explicitly endorsed by General Galvin.[40]

The question arises why, with so much support from forward-thinking commanders at all levels, this complex of ideas has been so slow to take? The answer, it seems, is twofold. First, much of the writing on the subject has had a flavor of good-life

---

[39]H. Afheldt, *Verteidigung und Frieden*, Munich: Hanser Verlag, 1976, and "Tactical Nuclear Weapons and European Security" in *Tactical Nuclear Weapons: European Perspectives*, Stockholm International Peace Research Institute, London: Taylor & Francis, 1978; E. Spannocchi and G. Brossollet, *Verteidigung ohne Schlacht*, Munich: Hanser Verlag, 1976; and H.J. Löser, *Raum-deckende Verteidigung*, Österreichische Militiärische Zeitschrift, Heft, no. 4, 1977.

[40]Richard E. Simpkins, *Race to the Swift*, London: Brasseys, 1985, p. 302.

technological utopianism. "Small is beautiful." Professional military folk have a profound suspicion of crankiness. There is a comfortable and reassuring solidity about a 50-ton tank, a self-propelled gun, an armored personnel carrier. A Harrier aircraft *looks* like a more dangerous machine than a helicopter. But a much more substantial reason lies in the fact that the onus for implementing most parts of such a concept—from obstacle creation to the provision of militia-type forces on the ground—would fall to the Federal Republic. Not until there has been a widespread conversion of both military and political opinion in that country can any movement take place. There are promising signs. The generation of commanders bred in the Wehrmacht has now wasted out. The concept of a non-nuclear, non-provocative, environmentally based defense might have an appeal across party boundaries and even to members of the Green Party. If so, the way might be open for an evolution in NATO doctrine comparable to, but even more far-reaching than the transition to flexible response. That took about 15 years. It is doubtful if, this time, we can afford to wait quite so long!

But which ever kind of development the future may bring, whether it be along the lines of ever higher and more expensive technology, or a more dispersed and decentralized local defensive network, or indeed both (for they are not necessarily mutually exclusive), two other imperatives will remain. The first is to promote a greater European defense identity. The second is to ensure a far greater compatibility between defense and arms control where conventional forces are concerned.

III. A European Defense Identity

The impetus for a European identity in defense arises directly from the nature of the Soviet threat, as analyzed earlier in this essay, with the corresponding need for Western Europe to maintain its self-confidence, self-respect and, above all, its political cohesion. This has led to the development of a number of institutional forums beginning with the Western European Union, which was established in 1954 as an expansion of the Brussels

Treaty Organization. Its membership since its inception has consisted of West Germany, France, Italy, the United Kingdom and the Benelux countries. Its aim is to further European integration and security through international cooperation. It has been greatly revitalized by the agreement at its 30th anniversary that foreign and defense ministers would meet twice yearly and that the WEU forum would be used to discuss defense questions as well as subjects such as arms control and disarmament, East-West relations, and European cooperation in weapons development. The advantage of the WEU is that it provides a specifically European but manageably small forum, which includes France, for discussion of security matters. Its assembly is the *only* parliamentary body mandated by treaty to discuss defense and security issues. It is barred by constitution from any operational military role. Its function is political with considerable emphasis on public information.

Within the European Community as a whole there has been provision since the Hague Summit of 1969 for what is known as European Political Cooperation. This provides for continuing and active consultation on a wide range of political issues, including European policy on East-West relations, the Middle East, and Central America. Coordination within EPC has played a vital role in maintaining a coherent Western approach in the various phases of the post-Helsinki process. But proposals, such as those made in 1981 by West Germany's Foreign Minister Hans-Dietrich Genscher and Italy's then-Foreign Minister Emilio Colombo, to extend the cooperation of Community members to include more military aspects of security have never been accepted, not least because one member, Ireland, does not belong to NATO and is neutral.

The Eurogroup was established within the NATO framework in 1968 at Great Britain's initiative following the Soviet invasion of Czechoslovakia and because of European concern about the Mansfield Amendment. All European members of NATO, except France and Iceland, are members. The Eurogroup promotes military cooperation in such areas as training, logistics, communications, medicine and long-term operational concepts. It also conducts an active information campaign particularly in North America.

Probably the most influential embodiment of the European identity is that devoted to equipment cooperation—i.e., the Independent European Program Group (IEPG), which consists of all the European members of the Alliance except Iceland. The case for collaboration in this field is well recognized and clear. It allows for better use of scarce facilities for research and development and cost-sharing. It leads to longer production runs, thus providing still further economies. It helps to achieve standardization and interoperability, thus improving military efficiency. Finally it demonstrates the cohesion of the Alliance and members' preparedness to work effectively together.

The difficulties of achieving a European defense identity are also well known. It is hard to reconcile operational requirements when nations operate in different environments with different tasks, different force structures, and different preferences arising from their past histories. Programs for equipment replacement are never exactly in step. The actual procedures for joint equipment procurement are time consuming and expensive. And there is an ingrained chauvinism in defense industries and ministries (much less so in armed forces), which takes much political effort to overcome. Despite all this there is a history of successful cooperation within NATO going back some 20 years.

Collaborative projects now account for about 15 percent of U.K. equipment expenditure, and most of the collaborative projects in question are European. This helps to preserve the European defense industrial base, which is important in economic terms and helps trans-Atlantic cooperation by providing the capability for a real European contribution. This is more important as we move into an era of ever higher technology, and ever greater equipment costs, as in the cases of SDI and ET.

The role of the IEPG was strengthened at the ministerial meeting in November 1984 by a directive stating that military staffs must work more closely toward harmonization of operational requirements and timescales; that all significant projects are to be referred to ministers at staff target stage; that rationalization of research and industrial resources is to be studied; and above all, nations should exercise greater discipline in not launching their own development proposals in competition with existing ones elsewhere, and should be more ready to adopt others' equipment if it is already in production. Pious hopes, perhaps? But at the same meeting agreement was reached to work cooperatively on a new heavy battle tank for the 1990s, a surface-to-air missile, and a military transport aircraft. All the thrust of recent political thinking is in the direction of giving more bite to the principle of arms cooperation, and it is unfair at this stage to be ultra-critical of slow progress.

IV. Arms Control

Quite obviously both the lines of possible future development toward a "less nuclear" defense posture could provide complications for arms control. Those associated with emerging technologies have been discussed earlier, together with possible means of circumventing them. A large-scale militia-guerrilla concept could lead to an increase in reserve forces, but these have never been included in arms control negotiations. If Liddell Hart's vision of a corresponding reduction in the size of the maneuver forces were realized, so much the better. But there is a much more fundamental point. For the past ten years the MBFR negotiations at Vienna on the reduction of conventional forces have been stalled—ostensibly on technical points concerning the number of forces within the area of interest and the methods of verifying any reductions. These are real enough. But in fact the talks have been stalled due to a lack of political will to make progress and for reasons that were mentioned at the outset.

The Soviet Union does not wish to reduce its conventional forces west of the Urals so long as they are worth their keep in holding the East European countries compliant and in buying some form of political purchase in the West. The West Europeans, for their part, supported the MBFR talks at the outset as a means of defusing Mansfield's initiatives. They support the talks now as a means of fending off Senator Nunn. A wiser course would be to explore a correlation of forces (to use the Soviet phrase) at lower levels than the present but still secure the essential interests of all parties. All have an interest—soon to become overriding—in saving money. The financial plight of

Western Europe, including the United Kingdom, was touched on earlier. Soviet interlocutors make no secret of their need to economize. The U.S. defense budget is also under increasing pressure, and the regime of steady real growth may already be at an end.

If so, an "MBFR solution" has everything to commend it. It could reduce the sense of military overhang experienced by the Europeans without diminishing the security of the Soviet Union's European empire. It could redound to the credit of the U.S. administration as a manifest contribution toward lessening the risk of war, if not toward directly raising the nuclear threshold. It might be simpler in conceptual terms and far simpler for verification if the lower force levels to be aimed at were denominated, not in round numbers of men and women, but in terms of formations (divisions, squadrons of aircraft), which are virtually self-counting and the composition of which is relatively stable.[41]

A further step might take the form of both sides agreeing that certain developments—probably in the area of emerging technology—should not be undertaken. It is now fairly generally agreed that, in the field of strategic systems, the introduction of multiple independently targeted re-entry vehicles by both sides has *reduced* stability at great expense. If they had been banned, by mutual agreement, under the first Strategic Arms Limitation Treaty (SALT I), everyone would have benefited. The same may now be true, for example, of systems designed for the deep attack of armored formations on the move. The technology, as already explained, is of mind-bending complexity. The expense will be high. Any gain for stability is highly questionable, since such systems, if they worked, would increase attrition, blur the nuclear threshold, and (because they are ostensibly offensive) seem provocative. It might be very much better for all if, under a self-denying ordinance, neither

---

[41]Warsaw Pact and NATO Divisions are not, of course, precisely equivalent in terms of combat. Differences could, however, be allowed for by a simple formula—given the will to make progress. Indeed there is no reason, in principle, why divisions could not be traded off against battlefield nuclear weapons, for example.

side were to field them. Such a measure would, for the Soviet Union, be self-verifying by the very nature of American society. For NATO it would be harder to verify but not necessarily impossible, if only the principle of on-site inspection of ammunition stocks could be conceded. Meanwhile there is everything to be gained from pressing for progress at the Conference on Disarmament in Europe in Stockholm on military security and confidence-building measures as a means of defusing the fear of surprise attacks.

V. Conclusions

From the whole of this tangled skein it may be useful to draw out a few conclusions. The first is the lesson to be learned by the European members of NATO from the exertions of Senator Nunn. It is to be hoped that he will not persevere with his congressional measures in their present form. But the emphasis he places upon basic provisions is wholly apropos. And the signs are that he is pushing upon an open door. So far as aircraft shelters are concerned, following the 1971–1974 European Defense Improvement Program initiated by the Europeans, some 70 percent of aircraft at NATO bases are now sheltered and more are planned. Special provision is being made under the latest NATO infrastructure agreement (itself a significant political achievement) for programs that support tactical air reinforcements including hardened aircraft shelters. Regarding ammunition, NATO defense ministers agreed in 1984 to improve critical holdings. As an example, the Federal Republic of Germany has increased spending on ammunition stocks by 13 percent in real terms between 1981 and 1984 and plans to sustain this rate of growth until 1987. Great Britain has earmarked funds over the next few years to improve stocks of anti-tank weapons and artillery and naval gun ammunition. It is important that these countries and the other European allies be held to these and similar undertakings. And there is need for much improvement in readiness, training and deployment, as well as in conventional equipment.

The second lesson has also been learned up to a point: the need for greater collaboration in equipment and procurement. This arises in part from the desire for better conventional defense, in part from the emerging technology studies and the potentially very high costs of implementation, and not least from Europeans' concern that unless they collaborate, American firms will sweep the board. But there is still far to go. It has been suggested, for example, that all projects costing more than a stipulated minimum (say, $250 million) should automatically be proposed for collaboration and that an agreement should be sought among the principal industrial allies to the effect that a limited number of larger projects will be put in competition between international consortia.

The third, and perhaps the most important, lesson concerns the need for a consensus-building exercise to work out the modalities of a new defensive concept—within the broad parameters of flexible response—that would combine new conventional technologies with the germinating notions of territorially based defense. This would provide for a force structure both more robust and more unambiguously defensive than anything we have seen since the days of trench-warfare, machine guns, and barbed wire. Whether it can also be cheaper depends, above all, on what type of bargain affecting conventional forces can be struck with the Soviet Union. None of this can be done quickly; but the need is urgent enough, and there is a great deal of work to be done. Let the start be made now.

Recent Publications of the Council on Foreign Relations

Trade Talks: America Better Listen!, C. Michael Aho and Jonathan David Aronson, Council on Foreign Relations, 1985.

Compact for African Development, Committee on African Development Strategies, Council on Foreign Relations in conjunction with the Overseas Development Council, 1985.

Latin Migration North: The Problem for U.S. Foreign Policy, Michael S. Teitelbaum, Council on Foreign Relations, 1985.

Third World Instability: Central America As A European-American Issue, Andrew J. Pierre, editor, Council on Foreign Relations, 1985.

India and the United States, Council on Foreign Relations, 1985.

Ripe for Resolution: Conflict and Intervention in Africa, I. William Zartman, Oxford University Press, 1985.

Arms and the African: The Military Influences on Africa's International Relations, William J. Foltz and Henry S. Bienen, eds., Yale University Press, 1985.

Canada and the United States: Enduring Friendship, Persistant Stress, John H. Sigler and Charles F. Doran, eds., Prentice-Hall, 1985.

A Changing Israel, Peter Grose, Vintage Books/Random House, 1985.

Prospects for Peace in the Middle East: The View From Israel, A Conference Report, Council on Foreign Relations, 1985.

For complete catalog and ordering information please contact Publications Office, Council on Foreign Relations, 58 East 68th Street, New York, N.Y., 10021. (212) 734–0400.